THE LITTLE BOOK OF DOGS

THE LITTLE BOOK OF DOGS

Virginie Bhat

CHÊNE

CONTENTS

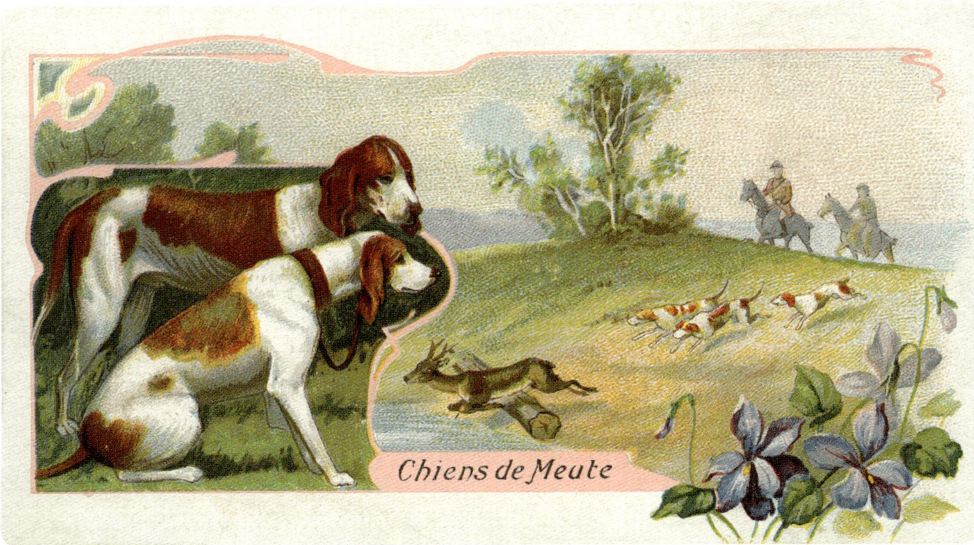
Chiens de Meute

THE STORY OF MAN'S BEST FRIEND

Like the grey wolf and golden jackal, the domestic dog belongs to the genus *Canis*, in the Canidae family. The first canids appeared about forty million years ago. Over thousands of years, with the changing climate and continental drift, these mammals evolved until one of them became the dog.

The origins of the dog

Although the dog has been considered man's best friend for thousands of years, there has always been uncertainty about the origins of a common ancestor. Science has long alternated between the wolf, the jackal and the fox, or even ruled them all out. In France, Georges Louis Leclerc de Buffon dismissed the connection with the wolf and fox in the eighteenth century. According to this naturalist, the dog's closest common ancestor was a 'shepherd dog'. This hypothesis of an original dog still appeals to some scientists, who think that the first dog physically resembled a dingo. Others are more drawn to the connection with the jackal or a cross between a wolf and a jackal. However, the hypothesis that the dog is descended from the grey wolf is the more commonly held among experts, which is why the dog species was given the Latin name Canis lupus familiaris (Canis lupus being a reference to the grey wolf). According to this theory, the wolf would have lived alongside humans. When, why and how?

Some authors believe that this took place between 100,000–400,000 years ago. However, there are still grey areas. A wolf is a wolf – it did not become a dog overnight. It would have taken a long time for the wild animal to turn into the pet we know today.

Of dogs, men and gods

Most scientists believe that the domestication of the dog began at the end of the Upper Palaeolithic period, long before that of other species. Archaeologists have found remains of primitive dogs in areas occupied by humans between 16,000–10,000 BC from the Iberian Peninsula to Siberia. Humans were still hunter-gatherers at that time. Wolves most likely would have approached them to steal the leftovers after hunts. Humans may have adopted wolf cubs, which they fed and then tamed. Hunter-gatherers settled during the Neolithic period. It was during this time that the wolf-dogs evolved. They adapted to human needs by becoming guard dogs, herding dogs, war dogs, draft animals and pets, among other things. Since then dogs have been held in such esteem that humans have sometimes given them a place on a par with their gods. In 3,000 BC, Anubis, the Egyptian god of the dead, had the head of a dog or a jackal, according to different interpretations. In Greek mythology, a monstrous, three-headed dog called Cerberus guarded the gates of the Underworld. In the Aztec religion, Xolotl was both the god of sunset and the dog-god who accompanied the sun into the Underworld. There are many examples, but two figures

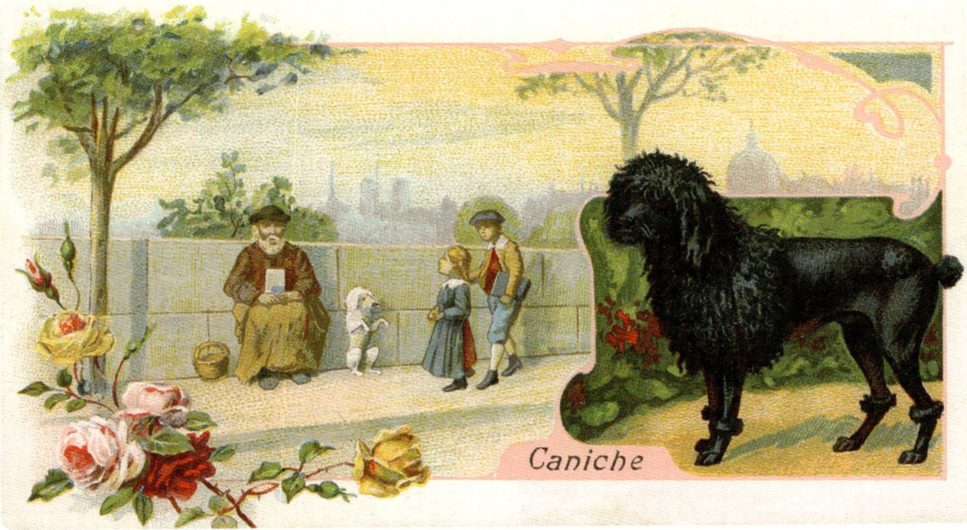
Caniche

stand out in the history of dogs. The first is that of the faithful companion, in the form of Argos, the dog Odysseus behind with his wife Penelope. The second is that of the monster that inhabits our nightmares or lives in the shadows, like the Hound of the Baskervilles.

An explosion of breeds

There are many uncertainties in canine history, and in the history of today's dog breeds too. However, both are tied to human history. Over the centuries, humans have modified the different breeds depending on the tasks we have entrusted them with. Lapdogs for the ladies of European and Asian courts; large,strong dogs to follow the armies of Alexander the Great and the Roman legions on their conquests; pack dogs to seek out game for Renaissance nobles out hunting; small, fast and agile dogs to hunt down rodents and pests in industrial towns, in the countryside and at ports; sheepdogs to accompany nomadic shepherds on their wanderings, and many others. There was literally an explosion of canine breeds in Europe in the nineteenth century. There were local and exotic breeds, brought back by Europeans from their conquests. By that time, selective breeding was no longer the preserve of the nobility - it was also of interest to scientists. The first dog shows were held in Britain, which was also where the first breed standards were established. France quickly followed suit and the first exhibition was held in Paris in 1863. The event, organized by the Imperial Zoological Society for Acclimatization, took place at the Jardin d'Acclimatation in the Bois de Boulogne. It brought together 850 dogs. The Société Centrale Canine was founded in 1881, and its public interest was recognized in 1914. Forty years later, a law was passed entrusting the society with managing the Livre des Origines Français (LOF), a breed registry also known as a stud book, which recognizes more than 300 French dog breeds. France is home to more than eight million dogs today, three-quarters of which are pedigree dogs.

FRENCH WATER DOG

Origin **France**

According to the French naturalist Buffon (1707-88), the French water dog originated in Spain or North Africa, where the climate gave rise to dogs with finer, silkier and longer hair than those of other regions. Dog experts today seem to reject this idea. Instead, they believe this dog originated in Central Europe, from where its ancestor went on to colonize Italy, France, Spain and Portugal. Whatever the case may be, it is a water dog. It loves water in all seasons, even in the coldest weather. This is the reason it is often used for hunting waterfowl. A worthy representative of this breed is often mentioned in history books: Moustache was the mascot of Napoleon's Vieux Grognards, veterans of his Imperial Guard. After many heroic deeds, he was killed by cannon fire on the battlefield, where he was buried with military honours. By the end of the Second World War, French water dog breeding was left in tatters and the breed had practically died out. Breeders reacted by crossing a poodle with water dogs from Spain, Portugal and Ireland to revive it. Today, this dog, with its long, woolly and curly hair, is a faithful companion for both hunters and families.

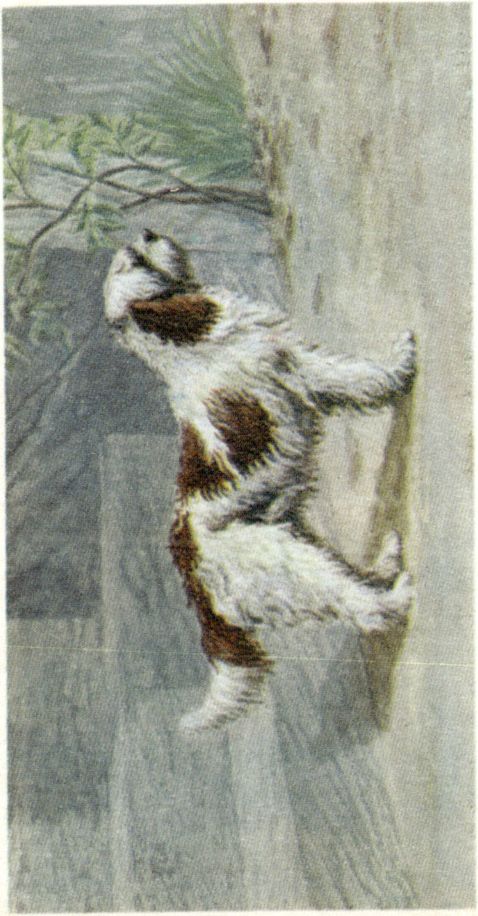

BORZOI

Origin **Russia**

The head of this Russian sighthound, which resembles a greyhound, is long and narrow, with a flat skull and long muzzle. It has a silky, wavy or curly coat, which is long on the body and short over the legs and sides. This graceful and elegant dog from the east had great appeal for the elegant ladies of Paris in the 1920s. One of these ladies, Countess Greffulhe, had a breeding kennel at the Château de Bois-Boudran, her country estate, which she started with a pair of borzois given to her by her friend Grand Duke Nicholas Nikolaevich in 1914. This member of the Russian imperial family had the best breeding kennel in Russia at the time. In his country, borzois were used by the nobility for hunting wolves. A pair of these hounds could stop a wolf in its flight, then hold it to the ground by its ears. After the Russian Revolution of 1917, the breed was forgotten, but not for very long. The Soviet Union rediscovered this infallible hunter and revived its breeding at the end of the Second World War. Today, borzois are kept mainly as pets rather than hunting dogs in western Europe and America.

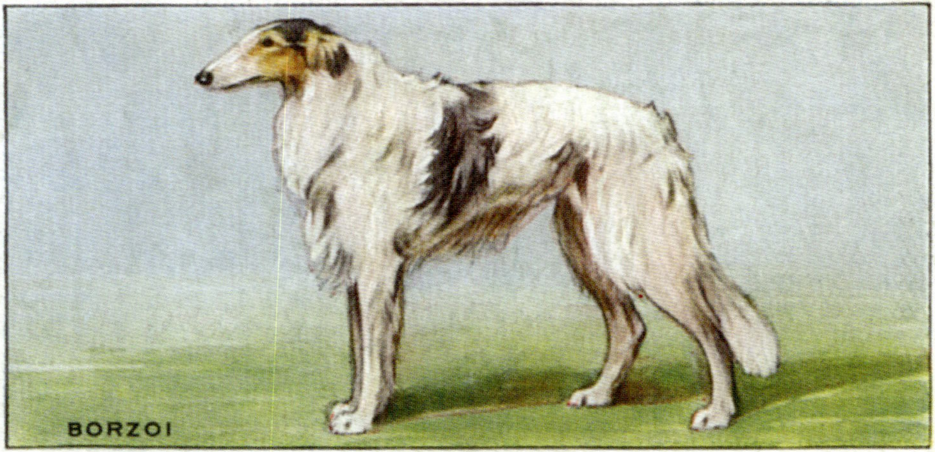
BORZOI

BASENJI

Origin **Central Africa**

Nobody has ever heard a basenji bark, because this dog only knows how to chuckle and sing. Even though its song, according to some, resembles Tyrolean yodelling, the basenji does not come from the coolness of the Alps, but from Africa. It is actually a very ancient breed, and it has even been depicted in Egyptian bas-reliefs. The basenji is recognized by its light frame, erect and pointed ears, and a curled tail. It is also known to have long accompanied the peoples of Africa on their hunts. At the end of the nineteenth century, Europeans took notice of this dog, with its proud bearing and almond-shaped black eyes, and brought back a few specimens from Africa. At the time, they were known as Congo terriers or African bush dogs. The breed was established in Europe by the two individuals brought back to Britain by Mrs Olivia Burns in 1936. The basenji today is sometimes thought of as a cat that does not know it, because it constantly grooms its short and silky coat. It is an intelligent and affectionate dog, and although it is independent, it does not like to be left alone. And if it sometimes has a puzzled expression on its face, it is because of the fine wrinkles that appear on its forehead when it pricks its ears.

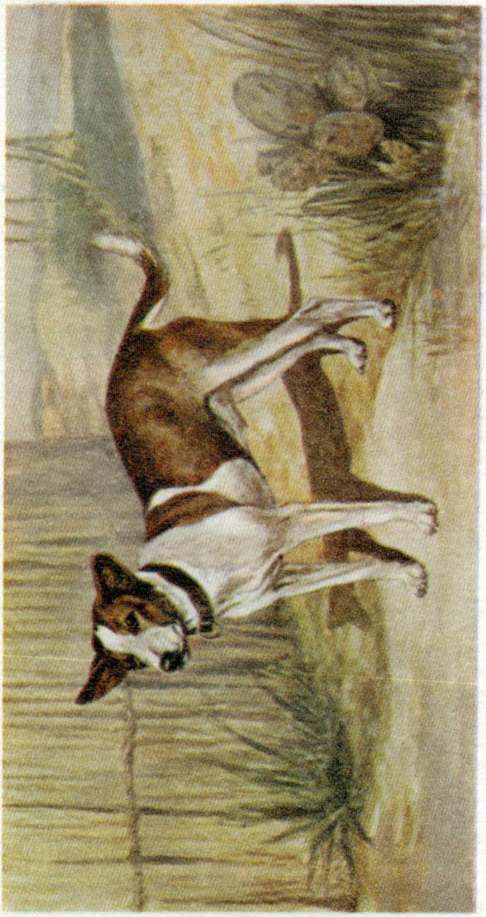

BLUE GASCONY BASSET

Origin **France**

There are three types of blue Gascony basset: the large blue, small blue and blue griffon. They all originated in the south of France. While their hair and sizes differ, they have in common a slate-blue coat and tan markings above their black eyebrows. The oldest of the three is the large blue Gascony basset, which is known to have hunted wolves, bears and wild boar with Gaston III, Count of Foix, in the fourteenth century. The blue Gascony basset is a hunting dog with a short, dense and coarse hair. Like its relatives, it has a keen sense of smell, which it uses mainly to track hares and rabbits. This breed might have died out at the end of the nineteenth century, had a handful of breeders not decided to revive it. Today, it has found its place in homes as a pet. Its boundless energy means it needs to be taken on regular walks in the countryside.

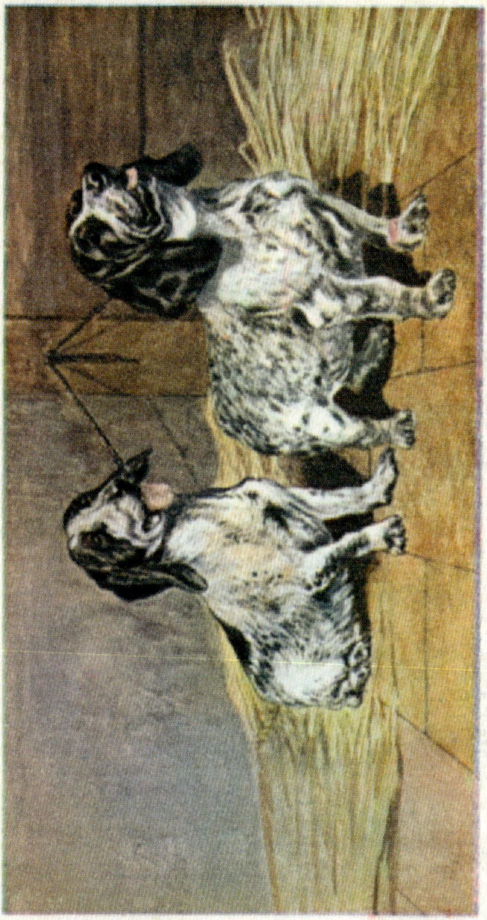

BASSET HOUND

Origin **Britain**

The basset hound has French ancestry: it is the result of crossing the Ardennais, Artésien and Normand basset breeds. In the nineteenth century, French emperor Napoleon III had two, a rough-coated one and a smooth-coated one. The latter was immortalized by the sculptor Emmanuel Frémiet in a bronze statue in 1853. During the same period, the British used this untiring hunter for their traditional fox hunts. The British set the standard for the breed – a smooth, short and close coat – in 1884, which is also why Britain is today considered the cradle of the basset hound. Originally a pack dog, the basset hound has short legs that can take it long distances. Its hanging skin, short hair, often tricolour coat and long, floppy ears give it a friendly appearance. However, it can be stubborn. Its gently, melancholy eyes would melt the hardest heart, but they are misleading; this dog is not sad, but a cheerful companion. The Hollywood cartoonist Tex Avery was able to to see through this. Droopy, the famous character he created in 1943, would constantly repeat in his deep voice: *'You know what? I'm happy.'*

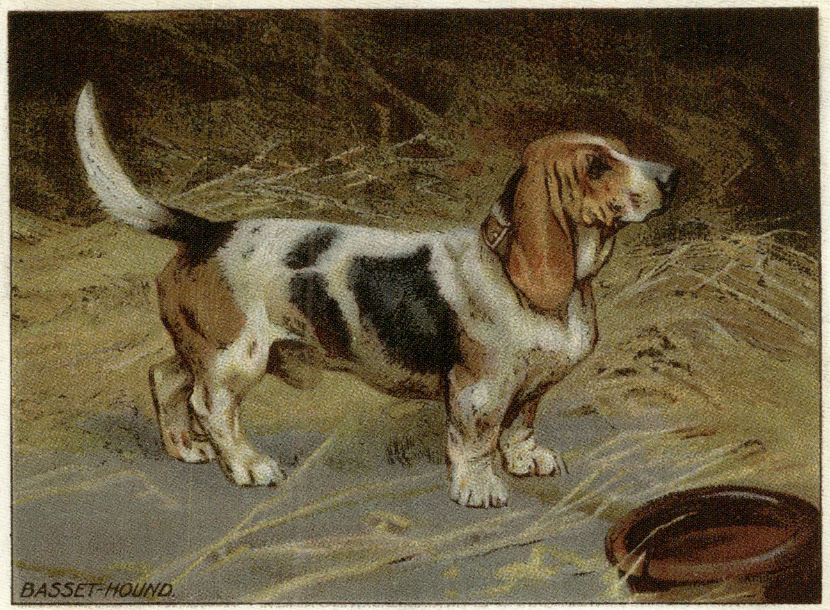

BASSET-HOUND.

BEAGLE

Origin **Britain**

While the beagle's history dates back to ancient Greece, the breed that we know today originated in Britain. However, the beagle would have had French roots, because they are believed to have arrived with the armies of William the Conqueror when he invaded England in the eleventh century. This dog today is an integral part of British traditions, to the extent that certain schools, such as Eton, have their own beagle kennels. The beagle is mainly used for hunting in France, where only one in ten dogs of this breed are kept as pets. It is also used as for sniffing out food at airports. Beagles are often tri-coloured, with black, white and brown coats. It is a cheerful and fearless dog, endowed with great energy. Friendly and ever alert, it is never aggressive or shy. Its completely round eyes and white-tipped tail, always wagging happily, are very appealing. Unfortunately, because it is not prone to hereditary diseases, the beagle has become the main breed of dog used in laboratory experiments on animals.

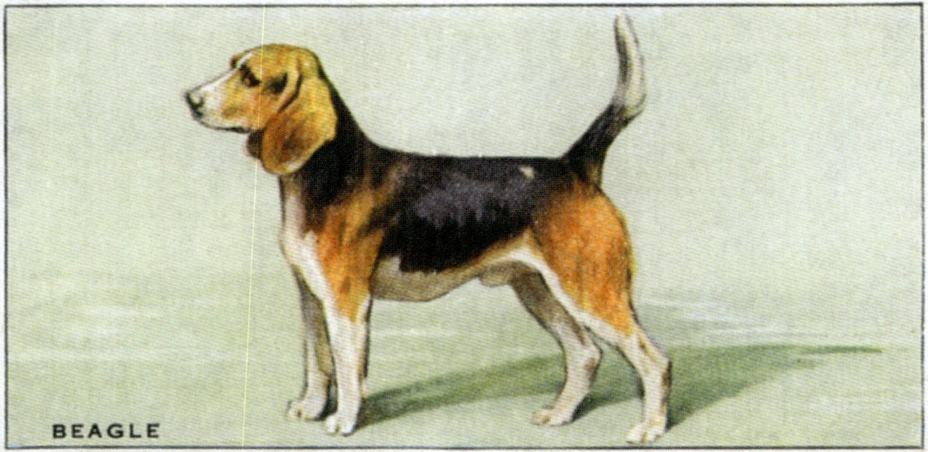
BEAGLE

BEDLINGTON TERRIER

Origin **Britain**

In the nineteenth century, miners in Bedlington, a town in north-east England, kept dogs to hunt rabbits or to rid the mines of rats. Among these dogs was the Rothbury terrier, which was no doubt crossed with a whippet to create the Bedlington terrier. This dog retains the body shape of a whippet, with its arched back and tucked-up belly. It has inherited its coat from the Rothbury terrier, which makes it resemble a lamb. Whether blue, liver or sandy, its coat is thick and linty and requires regular brushing and grooming. This dog is graceful, supple and muscular, but its pear-shaped head, topped with a fluffy white topknot, can come as a surprise. Today, this breed has left the mines to become a charming pet. The affectionate Bedlington terrier is good-natured. It is not keen on fighting; however, if called upon, this dog will not back down.

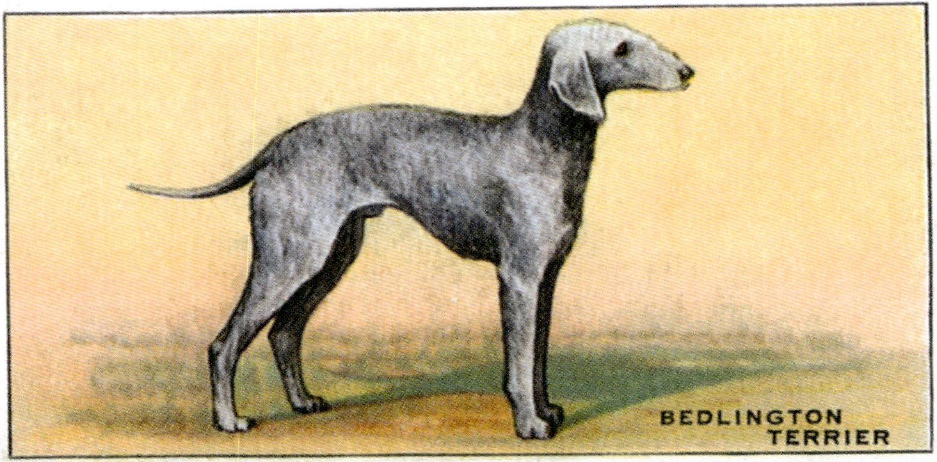
BEDLINGTON
TERRIER

GERMAN SHEPHERD

Origin **Germany**

The German shepherd, also known as the Alsatian, was once called a wolf dog, but it has no wolf genes. It is a breed created in its entirety by German dog breeders in the nineteenth century by crossing sheepdogs from central and southern Germany. A little after its creation, this dog was presented in a show and its breed standard was established. Its qualities - sense of smell, balance and sharp-sightedness - were all recognized and put to use. As a result, the German shepherd was recruited during the First World War to serve as a sentry, rescue dog and courier, and to detect poison gas. In the 1950s, it became famous through the success of the American television show *The Adventures of Rin Tin Tin*, which featured a brave, lively and loyal German shepherd that belonged to a small boy. The German shepherd has a double coat, which is short on the head and a little longer on the neck and behind the legs. There is also a long-haired German shepherd, which was officially recognized in January 2011. In addition to being the companion dog we know, the German shepherd is today also known for its role in searching through rubble, providing first aid and avalanche rescue, among other things.

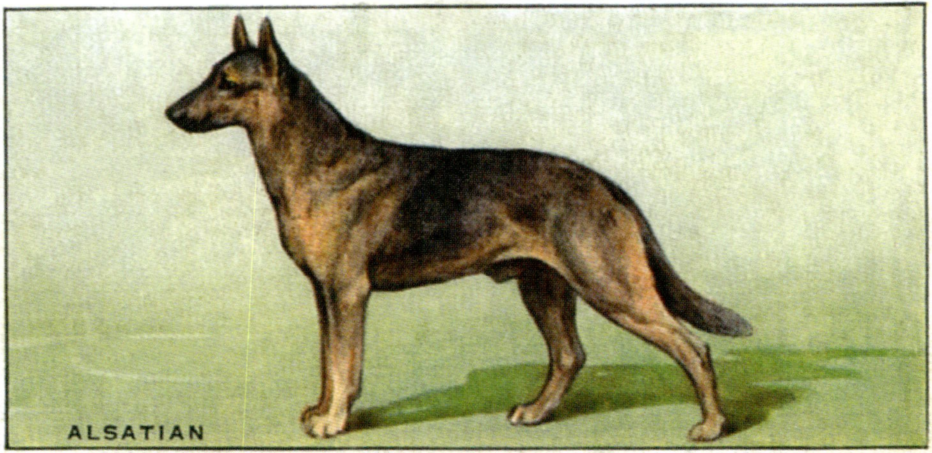
ALSATIAN

SOUTH RUSSIAN SHEPHERD

Origin **Russia**

This dog, also known as the South Russian ovtcharka, has protected flocks of sheep from wolves, bears and thieves since the eighteenth century in the Crimea, at the time located in southern Russia. It origins, however, remain a mystery. It is thought to be the result of mixing different breeds. It may be the result of crossing Spanish sheepdogs, which arrived in the Crimea with flocks of imported sheep, and strong Russian breeds that were capable of fighting bears and wolves, such as the Tartar or Caucasian sheepdog and the borzoi. During the Second World War, the breed was on the verge of extinction as a result of the destruction of the main breeding kennels. It would take the tenacity of a number of enthusiasts to revive the breed in the 1950s. The breed today is little known outside the borders of Russia, yet its elegant silhouette has great appeal. Its thick, coarse, bushy, and slightly wavy coat gives it a somewhat shaggy appearance. It is of equal length all over its body and measures from 10-15 centimetres. The South Russian shepherd's coat is most often white, or white and yellow, cream or grey. It can also be white with light grey markings or mottling.

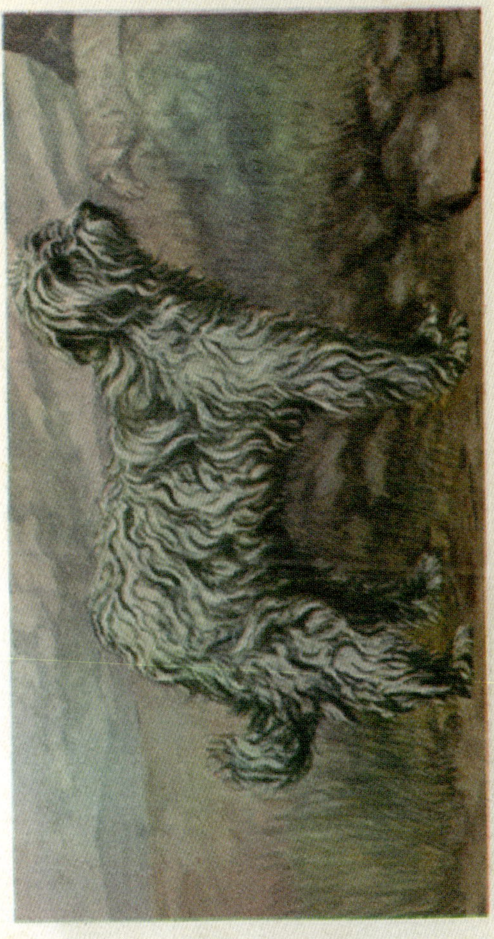

DUTCH SHEPHERD

Origin **Netherlands**

The sharp-sighted and hardy Dutch shepherd once guarded flocks of sheep on the undulating plains of the Netherlands. This strongly built dog comes from ancient stock and resembles the Belgian shepherd. The affectionate, docile and faithful breed would have died out at the end of the nineteenth century had it not been for the fans of the breed who created an association to preserve it. They are also responsible for the features of this dog, of which there are three accepted varieties: short hair, long hair and rough hair. The first is the most common, and the third is the rarest. Their coat can be blue-grey, salt-and-pepper, golden brindle or silvery. Today, because there are few flocks left to guard, the Dutch shepherd has been recruited for guarding and defence by the army and police force. Its devotion to its master also make it a good companion dog. Dog sports are a good outlet for the energy it has to spare.

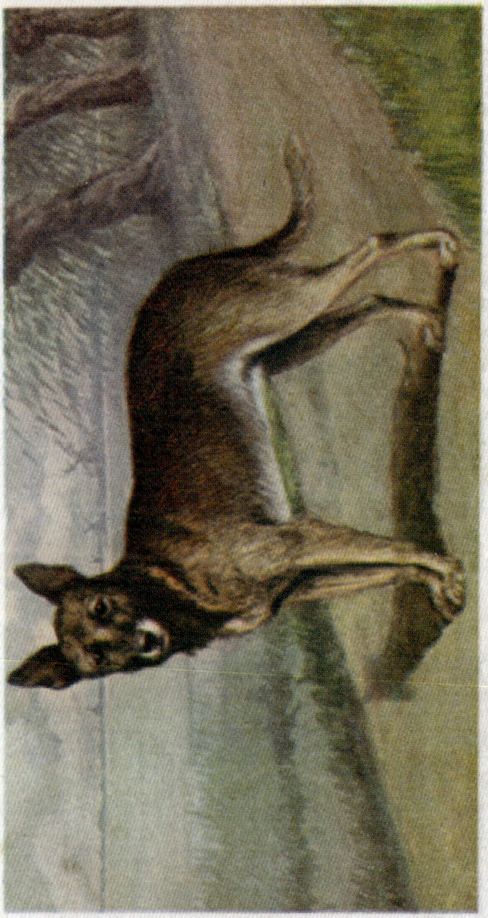

MALTESE

Origin **Mediterranean region**

Although dressed in a long coat, the Maltese has not always graced the homes of the elite. In ancient times, its ancestors were actually sturdy hunters, keeping warehouses and holds of ships free from rat and mouse infestations in ports and towns around the Mediterranean Sea. While it is certain that this breed originated in the Mediterranean region, it is not certain whether its name is derived from the island of Malta or Melita, modern-day Mljet, in the Adriatic Sea. The Maltese found great favour with western European nobility during the Middle Ages. It can be seen on the fifteenth-century tapestry *The Lady and the Unicorn*, and on paintings from the Renaissance, such as *Portrait of a Lady with a Lapdog* by Lorenzo Costa, dating from about 1500. It was around this time that the Maltese made its appearance at the court of Queen Elizabeth I of England. It was no doubt appreciated for the proud and distinguished bearing of its head. This small and intelligent dog barely weighs 4 kilograms at its heaviest and has a calm and reflective temperament. Lively and affectionate, it brings happiness to its masters.

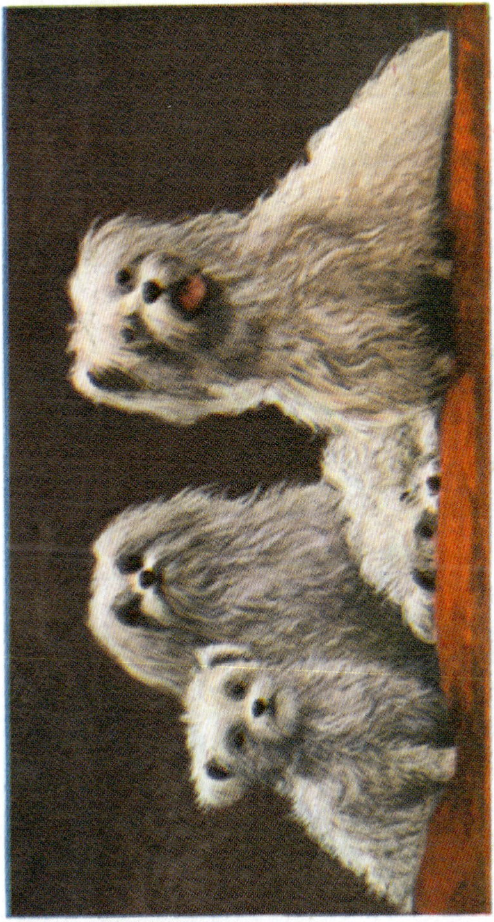

OLD ENGLISH SHEEPDOG

Origin **Britain**

The Old English sheepdog has been likened to a big teddy bear because of its gentle and swaying gait, which resembles that of a bear. It sturdy and square body is covered by a coarse, abundant and shaggy coat. It is grey and white in colour. It loves snuggling, to the point where it can become clingy. But the Old English sheepdog could not be further from a teddy bear, weighing as it does 35-40 kilograms. As its name suggests, it is an old British breed and it was once used to guard flocks of sheep. However, its origins remain uncertain. It may have accompanied Julius Caesar's Roman legions during his invasion of the island. It may also be the result of crossing European sheepdog breeds, such as the Caucasian sheepdog and the Italian Bergamasco shepherd. Whatever the case may be, the Old English sheepdog is intelligent and hardy. Although it can be born without a tail, if it is born with one, it is typically cut off at birth, according to English tradition. Its nickname, bobtail, reflects the custom of 'bobbing' or docking the tails of both horses and dogs, before being used for this particular breed. Today's breed standard accepts the presence of this appendage. The Old English sheepdog still holds true to its shepherding legacy, guarding its family just as its ancestors watched over their sheep.

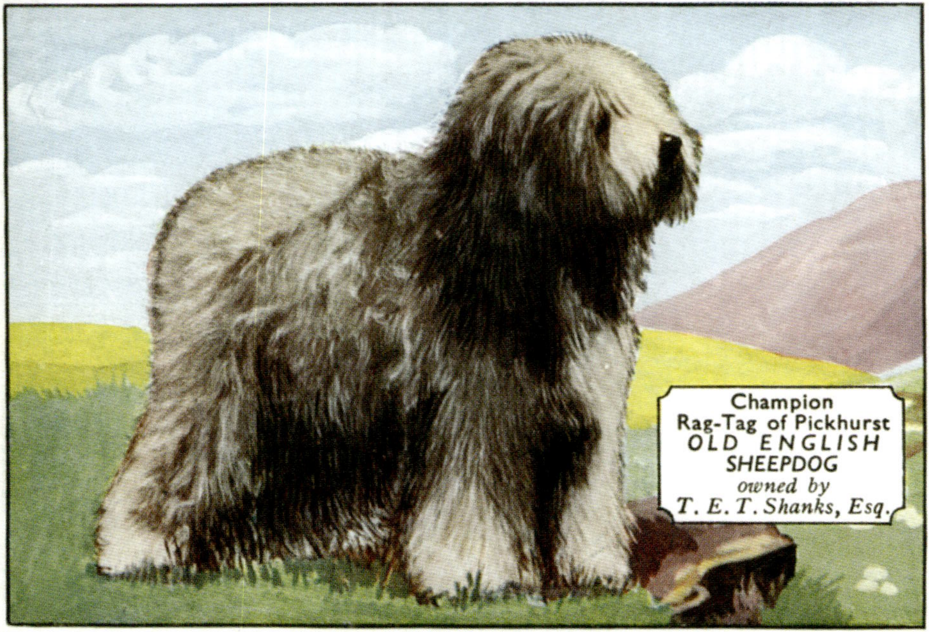
Champion
Rag-Tag of Pickhurst
OLD ENGLISH
SHEEPDOG
owned by
T. E. T. Shanks, Esq.

FRENCH BULLDOG

Origin **France**

In the Middle Ages, the butchers of Paris were already accompanied by mastiff-like dogs. They were used at the time to lead animals to the slaughterhouse. In the nineteenth century, they imported bulldogs from Britain, which they soon crossed with ratter dogs to produce a smaller breed, the French bulldog. The breed quickly became fashionable, its cocky appearance appealing to both ruffians – who used them as bodyguards – and the upper classes who frequented the Paris salons. The breed standard was definitively established in 1898. It was modified several times during the twentieth century, and now describes a dog that is strong and vivacious, despite its small size. Mainly comprising muscle mass, the French bulldog weighs 8–14 kilograms. It has a brown coat, which may be brindled, and it has a naturally short tail. This dog today is still very urban. However, it needs to be exercised without running, which it inadvisable given its limited breathing capacity.

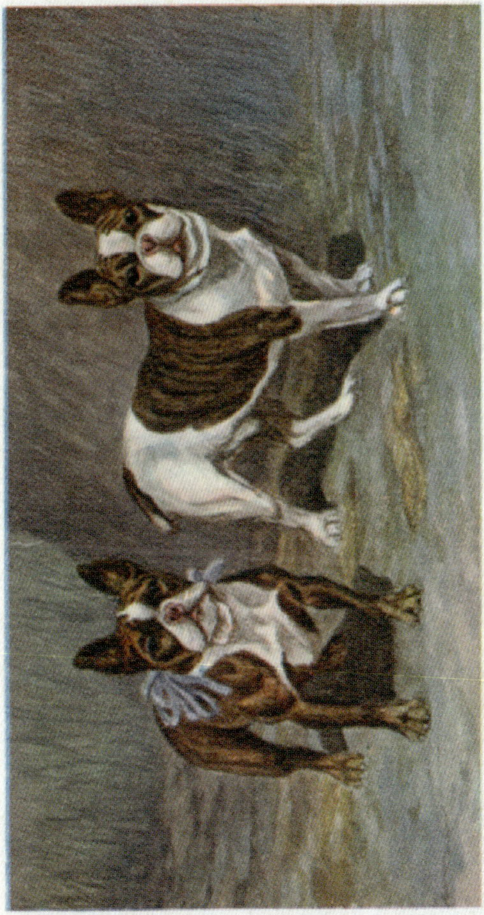

APPENZELLER CATTLE DOG

Origin **Switzerland**

There is no doubt that this dog has long been used to herd cattle around the small Swiss town of Appenzell. However, the first ever reference to it came in 1853 in the book by Friedrich von Tschudi, *Tierleben der Alpenwelt* (Animal Life in the Alps). It was described as a 'short-haired cattle dog of various colours, of medium size and with a clear voice'. In 1895, the head forester Max Sieber was concerned by the rarity of this hardy and lively breed and asked the Swiss Canine Society to preserve it. Three years later, the canton of Saint Gallen became committed to the preservation of this dog, which was recognized and won awards at dog shows shortly afterwards. Since then, the Appenzeller cattle dog breeders have strived to ensure the survival of the breed. Today, this dog is considered a trustworthy guardian. It has a black or havana-brown coat, with symmetrical tan or white markings. On its wedge-shaped head, a white blaze or strip runs between the top of the skull and the muzzle. This intelligent and fun-loving cattle dog loves the great outdoors above all.

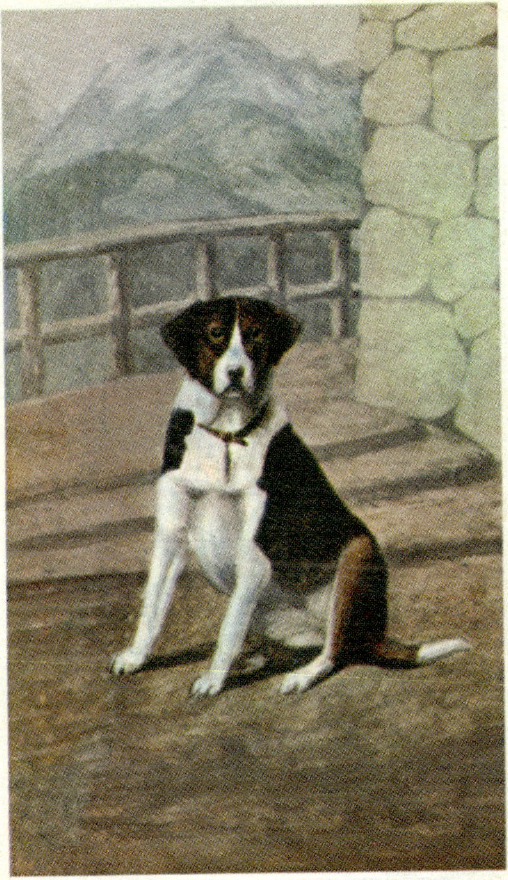

ARIÈGE POINTER

Origin **France**

The Ariège region was the birthplace of two hunting dogs, the Ariège pointer and the Ariegeois. Although the two breeds co-existed in the same area, they were not used by humans for the same purpose. The first was a pointing dog, the second a scent hound. The Ariège pointer is larger than the Aregeois. Its coat is white, ticked with pale orange or with brown flecks, while its cousin is white with black markings. What they have in common is a keen sense of smell, and elegance. The orange and white dog with lean legs and prominent musculature painted by Jean-Baptiste Oudry in the seventeenth century may have been an Ariège pointer in its early days, unless it was the result of cross-breeding carried out in the nineteenth century between the old French pointer and southern pointing dogs with orange and white coats. Long prized by hunters, the Ariège pointer practically disappeared after the Second World War. By 1964, there were no Ariège pointers listed by the Société Centrale Canine on its LOF breed registry. In 1989, a handful of breeders were concerned by this and decided to revive this hunting dog. They were successful, with 47 dogs registered in the LOF in 2010.

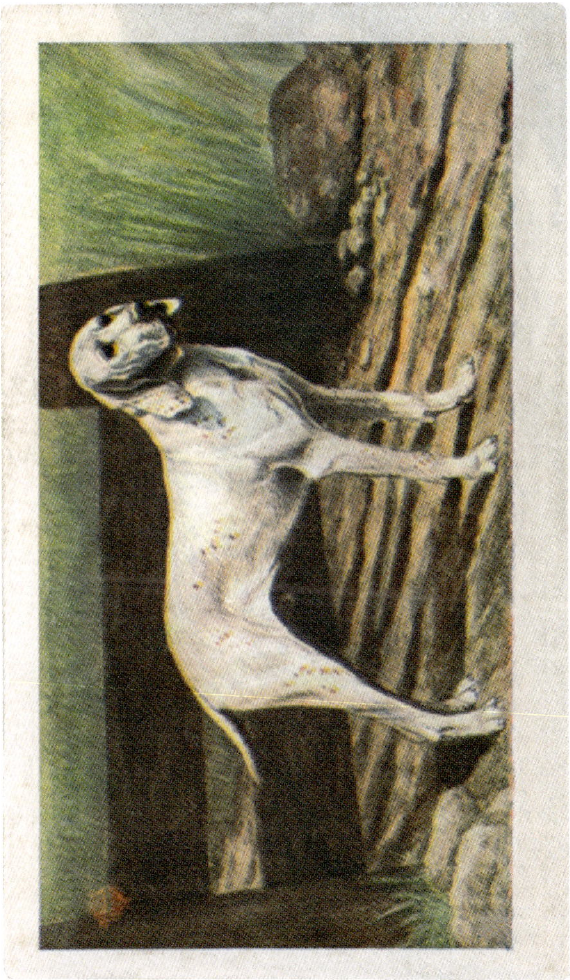

BOURBONNAIS POINTER

Origin **France**

This pointing dog has been around for a long time, a fact that can be seen in its name, which comes from the former Bourbonnais region, today the French department of Allier. It was mentioned in the writings of Ulisse Aldrovandi in the sixteenth century. This Italian naturalist referred to it at the time by the Latin name *Canis burbonensis*. He described it as a spotted dog with a short tail that was good at catching quails. This pointer is mostly born without a tail, and more rarely with a stump. Hunters describe it as a good, rustic hunting companion. The Bourbonnais pointer can have a fawn or brown coat, colours that were once expressed in more flowery language: 'peach flower' for the former, and 'faded lilacs' or 'wine lees' for the latter. This dog, with its sweet and expressive look, was included in the LOF breed registry until 1963, when it disappeared for ten years. In 1970, a group of enthusiasts scoured the countryside in search of dogs that even remotely resembled the ancient breed. Somehow they managed to find a core of specimens with which to revive it. Among them was Rasteau, son of Joséphine and Napoléon, German pointers once owned by the singer Pierre Perret.

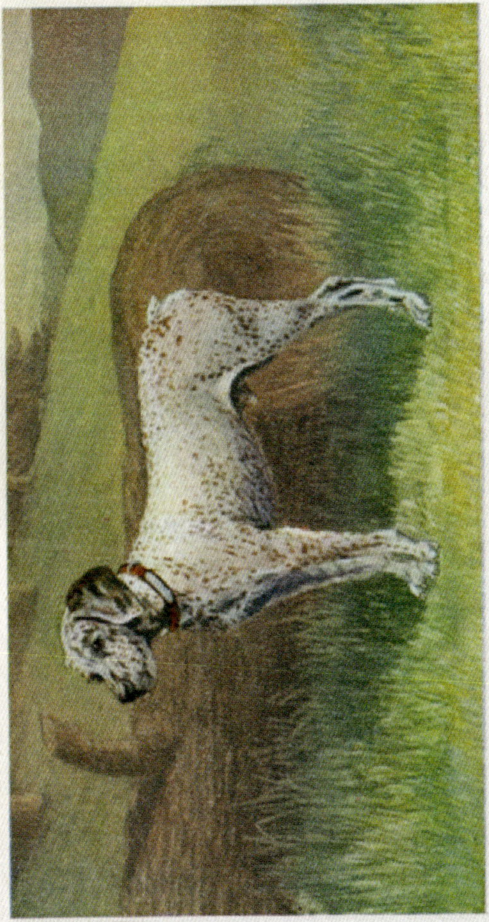

DUPUY POINTER

Origin **France**

The Dupuy brothers gave their name to this breed, which they created in 1815. The two hunters considered their Poitevin pointers to be a little two heavy for their pastime, so they decided to lighten their dogs' frame through cross-breeding. They chose to cross their bitch with an English greyhound. After selecting puppies and further selective breeding, the new breed was definitively created. The Dupuy pointer inherited its superb talent for distinction from its English forebear and its keen sense of smell from its French ancestors. The breed standard was introduced in 1963, and described a long, narrow, fine and lean head. The slender male could grow up to 67–68 centimetres tall. Its golden or brown eyes were sweet and dreamy. Its neck was long, rounded and thin. Its hair was always smooth and relatively short. Its coat was dark brown and white, sometimes spotted. Unfortunately, barely twenty years after its creation, the dog was already endangered as hunters preferred other companions. The Dupuy pointer appears to have died out today.

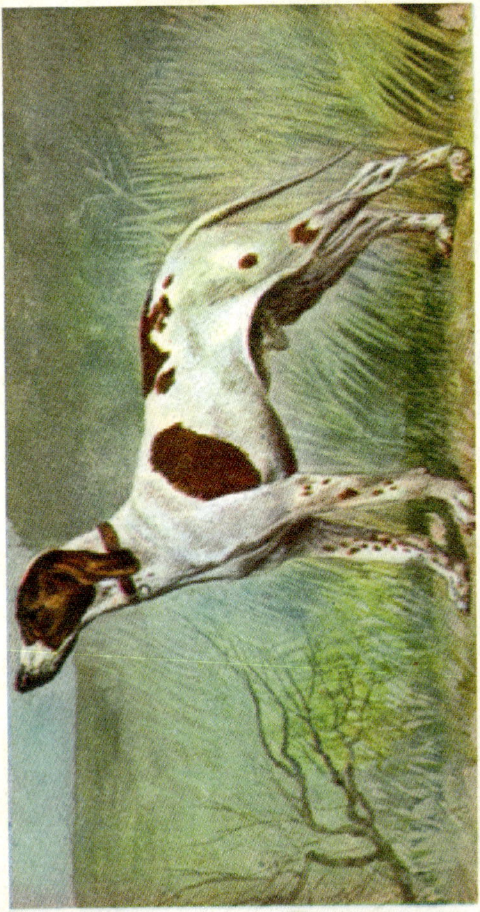

FRENCH POINTER

Origin **France**

The French pointer descends from a long line of pointing dogs that the famous Count of Foix, Gaston Phébus, described in his fourteenth-century *Livre de la Chasse* (Hunting Book). Originating in the south of France, this elegant dog was present at every hunt, from the hunting parties of the aristocracy to the humblest poaching expeditions. It is also known as the Charles X pointer. It is said that this French king, brother and successor to Louis XVI, was a compulsive hunter who owned several hunting packs. Two types of French pointers were later bred, the Gascon French pointer and the Pyrenean French pointer. Both have the same temperament: gently responsive to their masters' affection, docile, calm and faithful. Both are well suited to all terrains, when hunting or playing. They have a good sense of smell and are good with children. They easily adapt to urban life, especially if introduced to it at an early age. These very sensitive dogs are intolerant of unfairness and cruelty. Their coat is brown or brown and white - sometimes spotted - or brown with fawn markings. The Gascon French pointer is the stronger of the two variants. Its smaller, lighter and more muscular Pyrenean cousin has been so successful that it has outshone the former.

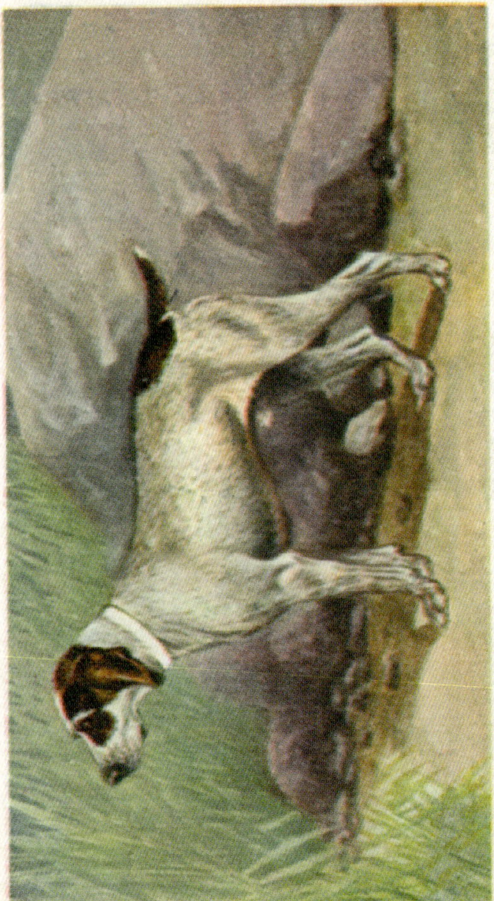

BULLDOG

Origin **Britain**

The bulldog has not always been a dog of the English high society. In the early nineteenth century, it was still used to bait bulls in front of roaring crowds. When these events were banned in 1835, breeders began to modify their silhouette by selective breeding. From a powerful dog, the bulldog became small and squat. This new appearance quickly appealed to the British at dog shows in the late nineteenth century, which allowed the dog to become the symbol of Great Britain, just as the cockerel has come to represent France. It is also often associated with John Bull, a character invented in 1712, who is to the United Kingdom what Uncle Sam is to the United States. Despite its grumpy expression, the bulldog has a heart of gold. Its short muscular legs can reach surprising bursts of speed. Its stocky body gives it the air of playing hard. However, it is so sensitive that reprimands stop it in its tracks. The bulldog is also a generous, brave, devoted and tranquil companion.

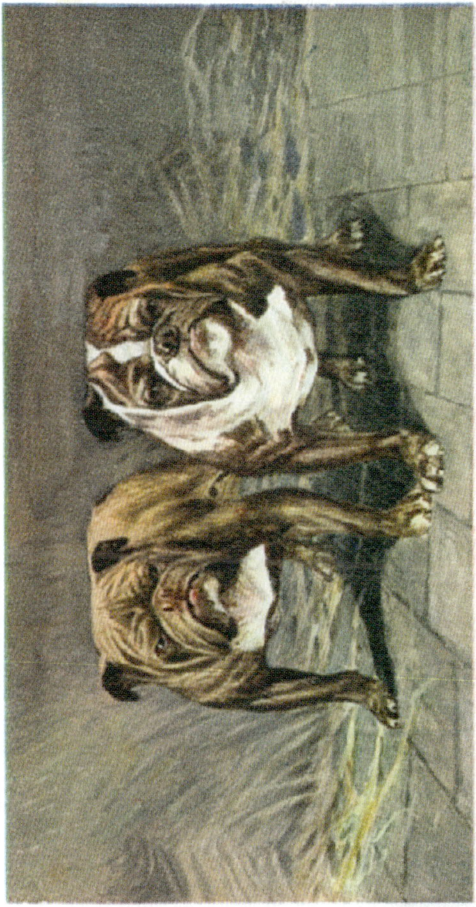

BULLMASTIFF

Origin **Britain**

In the Middle Ages, the English used large and powerful dogs to defend their property and livestock. Among these was the mastiff, which, when crossed with the bulldog, gave rise to the bullmastiff. This dog has such strength that it was quickly destined for guard duties. In the nineteenth century it was used to accompany gamekeepers to track down poachers. Its brindled or fawn coat also made it easy to camouflage in the darkness. It would chase and bring down a poacher, then wait for its master before releasing him. This work led to it being nicknamed the 'gamekeeper's night-dog'. Despite its great strength, this black-masked dog is not aggressive. However, it can demonstrate its dominance to any companion dogs. Therefore, it should be introduced to them at a very early age. The bullmastiff today has become a pet in many homes. Intelligent and cheerful, its is devoted to the members of its family.

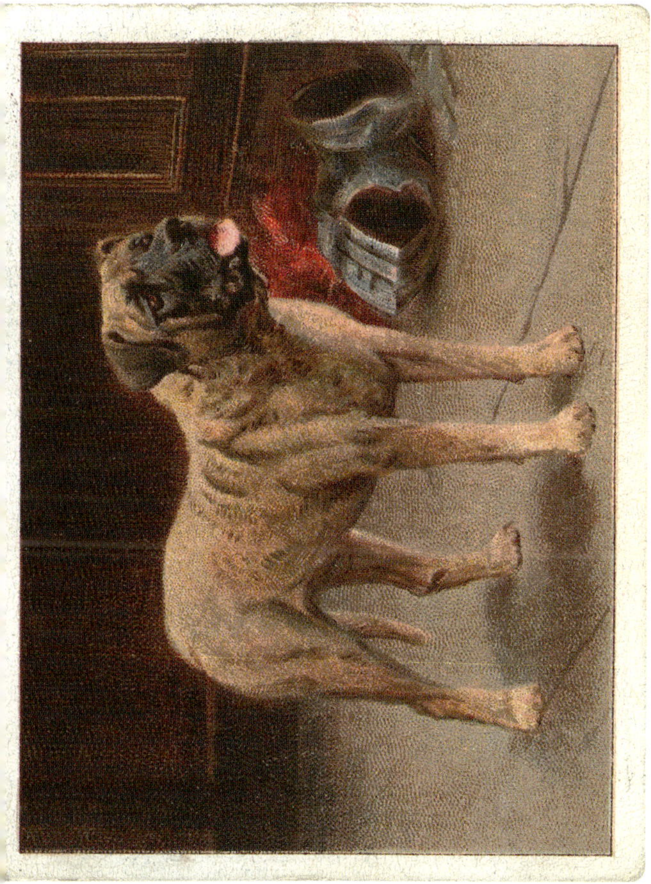

BULL TERRIER

Origin **Britain**

The bull terrier is the quintessential English canine gladiator. Originating in England in the thirteenth century, it was selectively bred after crossing a bulldog with a terrier for the purpose of taking part in bull, bear and horse-baiting events. When those popular blood sports were banned in 1835, dog breeders continued to preserve the breed. From a fighting dog, the bull terrier became a show dog. One of the most famous breeders was no doubt James Hinks, of Birmingham. According to canine history, he crossed bull terriers with Dalmatians and greyhounds to give the breed more elegant features. The result of this selective breeding was the bull terrier's oval head; another was its immaculate white coat. Although is has long remained fashionable, this colouring gave way to others in the twentieth century. The breed standard does not specify a weight or size. Only the miniature bull terrier should not exceed 35.5 centimetres at the withers, the highest point of its body at the top of the shoulder blades. Today, the bull terrier makes a very good companion. It naturally tends to dislike being alone, so it must be accustomed to it from an early age. Lively and tenacious, it loves exercise... and naps on the sofa.

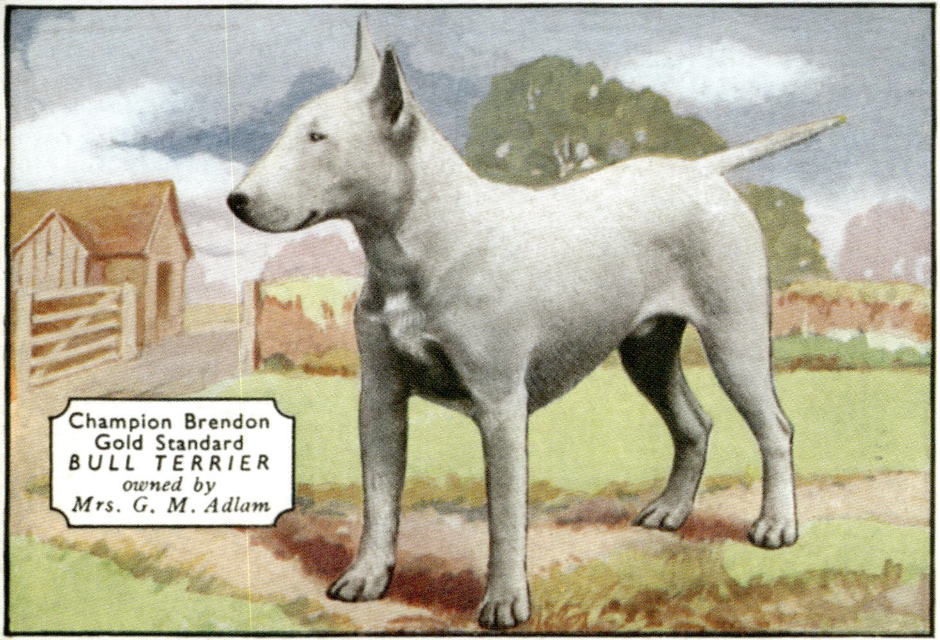
Champion Brendon
Gold Standard
BULL TERRIER
owned by
Mrs. G. M. Adlam

CAIRN TERRIER
Origin **Britain**

This is an ancient breed of pure Scottish stock. In the fifteenth century, the Scots made use of its qualities for hunting, particularly rabbit and hares on rocky terrain. The name cairn is a reference to the piles of stones that characterize that landscape. In the seventeenth century, King James IV of Scotland presented a few individuals to French king Louis XIII, where they were known as *chiens terrards*. The cairn terrier competed for the first time in a dog show in Britain in 1908, and it was officially recognized as a breed three years later. France would have to wait until the 1930s to see the first specimens; and it was probably thanks to Toto, a cairn terrier that starred in the famous musical film *The Wizard of Oz* (1939) that the breed became known the world over at the end of that decade. The cheerful and intelligent cairn terrier has a pretty face, with pointed ears and sparkling dark hazel eyes. It has a double coat that protects against harsh weather and undergrowth. Its thick hair varies in colour from cream to grey, by way of red and sand. Its short tail wags merrily. Weighing 6-7.5 kilograms, the cairn terrier is an energetic and strong-willed dog. Its highly sociable temperament has made it a popular pet.

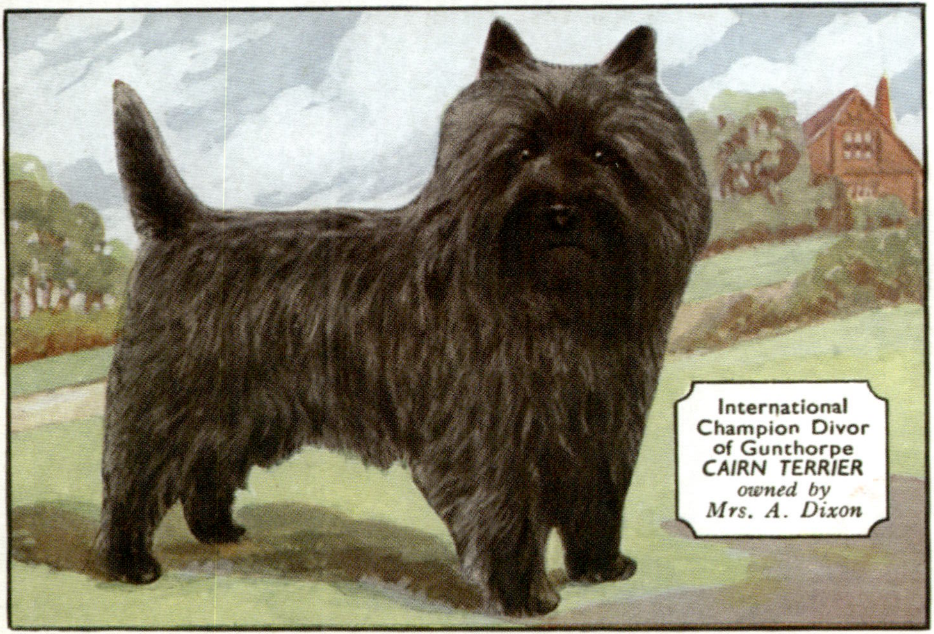
International
Champion Divor
of Gunthorpe
CAIRN TERRIER
owned by
Mrs. A. Dixon

POODLE

Origin **France**

In the sixteenth century, the forebears of the poodle were called *barbets*. Those dogs especially loved to splash in brackish marshes and hunt birds, mainly woodcocks. It was at that time when the best duck hunters began to be selectively bred. These new dogs, which were excellent swimmers, were then given the name 'duck dogs', or canichons, from where their French name, caniche, is derived. In the sixteenth century, the first individuals made their appearance in high society, where this gently and affectionate breed won great favour with the ladies. Two centuries later, the court of King Louis XIV became infatuated with the first miniature poodles, which were lively and intelligent. The poodle family today is a large one. The different varieties are classified by size, coat and colour. The French breed standard precisely sets out all characteristics and defines the authorized coat clips for shows: lion clip, modern clip and English clip. According to this standard, the standard poodle measures 45-60 centimetres tall; the medium poodle, 35-45 centimetres; and the miniature poodle, 28-35 centimetres. Toy poodles cannot exceed 28 centimetres. Poodles can have a black, white, brown, grey or orange fawn (apricot) coat, which can be frizzy, curly or corded.

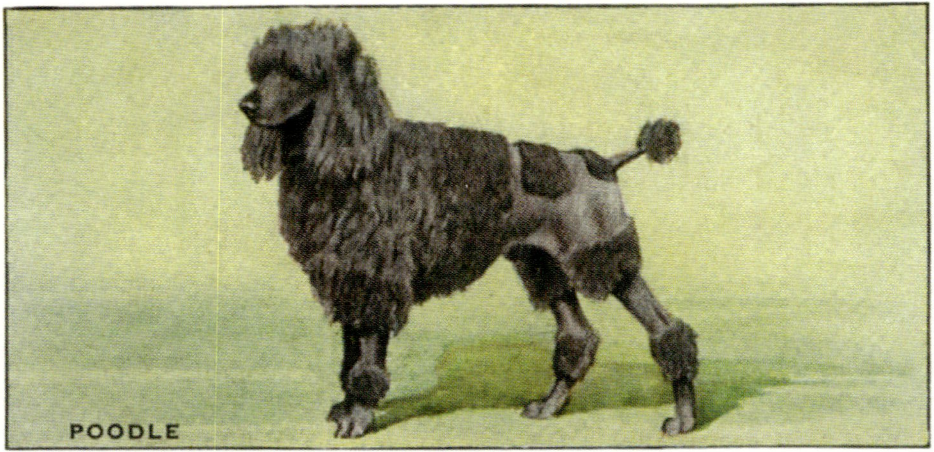

POODLE

CORDED POODLE

Origin **France**

Although it was very common until the nineteenth century, the corded poodle has become quite rare today. It has a thick coat with a fine, woolly and dense texture, forming cords which should measure at least 20 centimetres. The standard for this dog was adopted in 1936. In the same year, the Fédération Cynophile Internationale (World Canine Organization) recognized France as the country of origin, even though it had been suggested at the time that poodles originated in Germany. Like all poodles, the corded poodle loves water and possesses a very good sense of smell; certain poodles are used today to sniff out drugs and explosives. Although it was a typical dog in French homes for many years, the poodle ceded its place to the labrador in the 2000s.

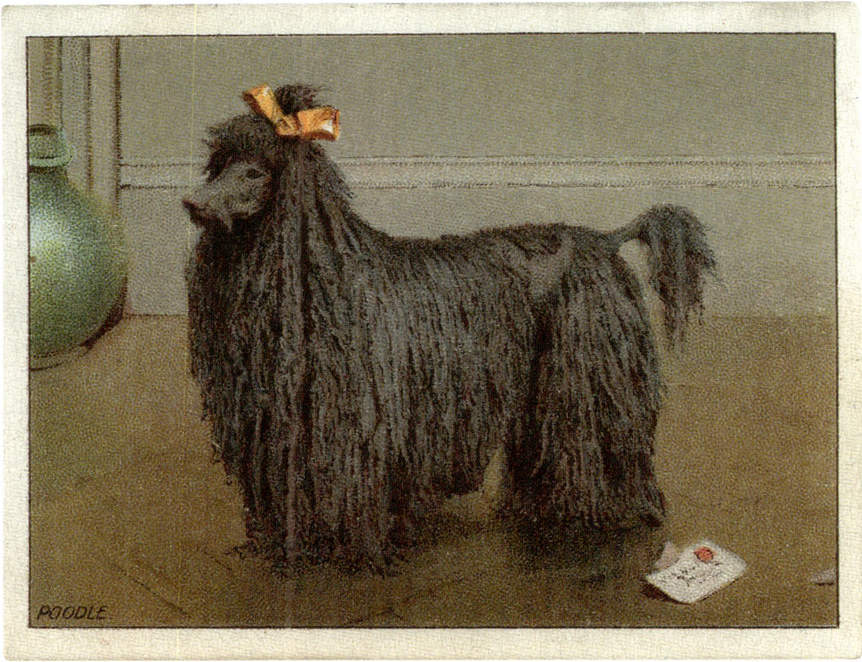
POODLE.

OTTERHOUND

Origin **Britain**

For many years this dog accompanied its master on the hunt for otters. However, after measures were implemented to protect the European otter in Britain in the 1960s, this breed is dying out. Births are declining every year: only 28 were recorded in 2011. This hunting dog has not yet found a way to appeal to families as a pet. However, it has a good and even temperament. It is a sturdy dog with long, dense and coarse hair. Its majestic head holds sparkling and intelligent eyes. A particular trait of this breed is its long, pendulous ears with folds that give them an interesting draped appearance. The otterhound loves running over firm ground after leaving the water. Its ancestors may have been English hunting dogs with a hint of French griffon. It has inherited their bravery and tenacity.

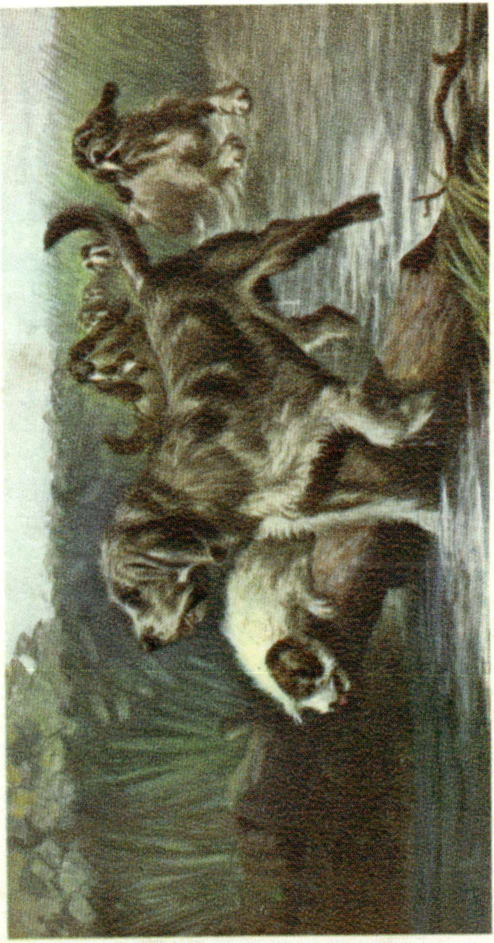

RUSSIAN HOUND

Origin **Russia**

There is no reason why the borzoi should outshine other Russian dogs. There are many kinds – hunting dogs, guard dogs and companion dogs. Among these, the Russian hound appeared in the country in the late eighteenth century. It was a hunting dog with a keen nose; hares and foxes were its main quarries. In traditional hunts, it was used together with the borzoi. As part of a pack, its role was to flush out the quarry and drive it back towards its master. Its deep and melodious voice allowed men to follow in its path. In the nineteenth century, Russian breeders embarked on a severe selection process in order to standardize for the breed, but this only succeeded in 1925. Today, they continue the quest for international recognition, which does not seem likely. Nonetheless, the Russian hound is an appealing breed. It has a medium height and measures 60–68 centimetres at the withers. Its hair is quite short and dense, and its coat has a fawn colouring with white markings. It has a large and strong head with triangular ears. This loyal and affectionate dog will one day leave the hunting pack to become an adorable companion for life. Like all hunting dogs, it has a lot of energy, which it burns up on long walks.

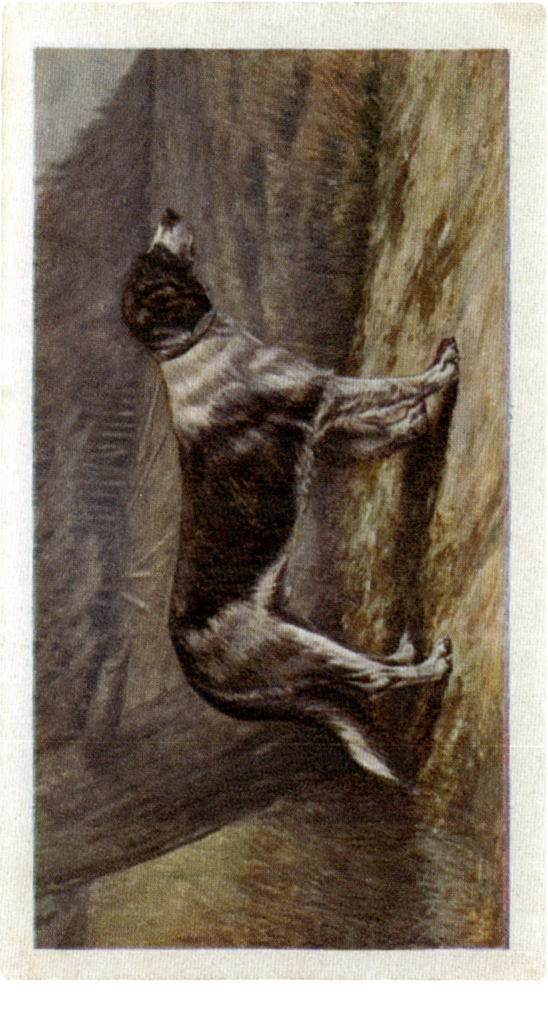

GERMAN POINTER

Origin **Germany**

The wirehaired pointer first appeared in in Germany in the nineteenth century. It was created by less well-off hunters who were seeking an all-purpose breed of dog suited to all types of hunting and terrain. After a number of different crosses, particularly with the korthals griffon and the roughhaired pointer, they ended up with a dog with dense, wiry hair that formed a coat that could withstand the harshest of weather conditions. They named this new breed of hound the drahthaar, 'wire hair'. This dog's qualities soon appealed to German hunters, followed by French hunters, who also began to use them. Today there are three related variants of the German pointer: the German wire-haired (drahthaar) pointer, German long-haired (langhaar) pointer and German rough-haired (stichelhaar) pointer. There is also another German pointing dog known as the German shorthaired pointer. It is better known than the others. The four breeds share the same passion: hunting. The energetic, self-controlled and balanced German pointer has an elegant silhouette. Its prominent eyebrows, whiskers and beard enhance the energetic aspect of its head. This dog forms a close attachment to its master.

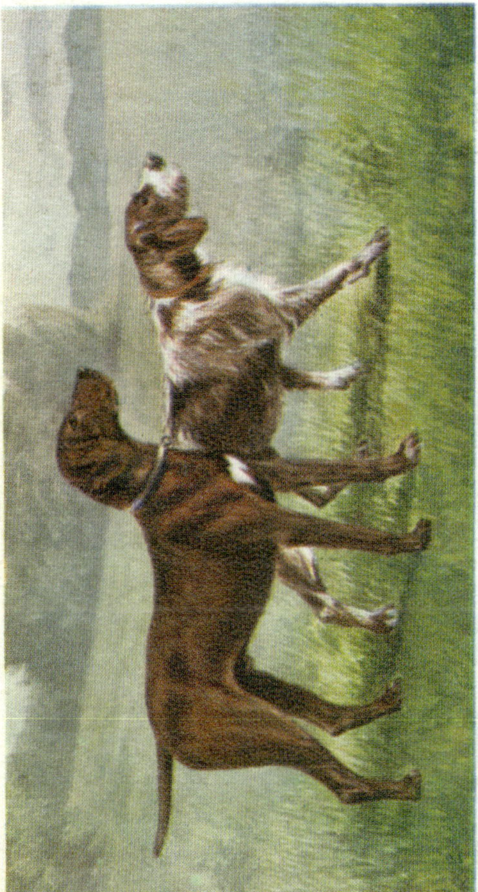

SWEDISH ELKHOUND

Origin **Sweden**

Elkhounds originated in Scandinavia. They would often accompany their masters when hunting European elk, also known as moose, in Sweden and Norway. These dogs could also be used to hunt bears and lynxes. In 1946, both Sweden and Norway decided to differentiate their own breeds, which canine associations had judged to be the same until that time. The Swedes called their dog the jämthund, after the name of a province in the centre of the country, Jämtland. This dog has a silhouette marked by its hunting work, and is sturdy and strong. It has a grey overcoat, which is short on the head and longer on the the chest, and a short and soft undercoat, preferably cream coloured. This thick coat allows it to cope with icy winters. The Norwegian elkhound is smaller, and there are two varieties, the grey and the black elkhound. The grey Norwegian elkhound sailed with the Vikings. Their remains have been found in the graves of these fierce fighters in the south-west of Norway.

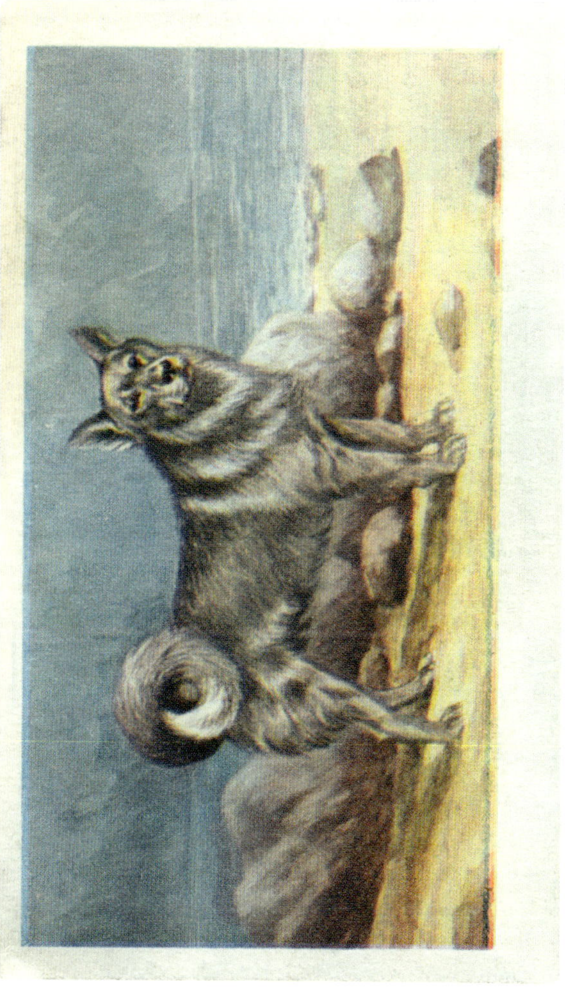

LEONBERGER

Origin **Germany**

This breed of dog has an uncertain background. It is believed to have appeared in the German town of Leonberg in the nineteenth century, the creation of one of the town councillors, Heinrich Essig, whose aim was to produce a dog that resembled the emblem of the town, the lion. He began the breeding process by crossing a black-and-white Newfoundland female with a male Saint Bernard. After this first cross, Essig persisted with his quest by drawing on the genes of Pyrrenean dogs. The result of those cross-breeding activities was large dogs with predominantly long white coats. The first Leonberger was finally 'born' in 1846. This recent breed is strong, robust and elegant. A male can weigh up to 60 kilograms. Its coat, which varies in colouring from lion yellow to dark fawn, is enhanced by a black mask. Its intelligence, self-assurance and sociable temperament make it appealing to families. It is even described by some as quite clingy.

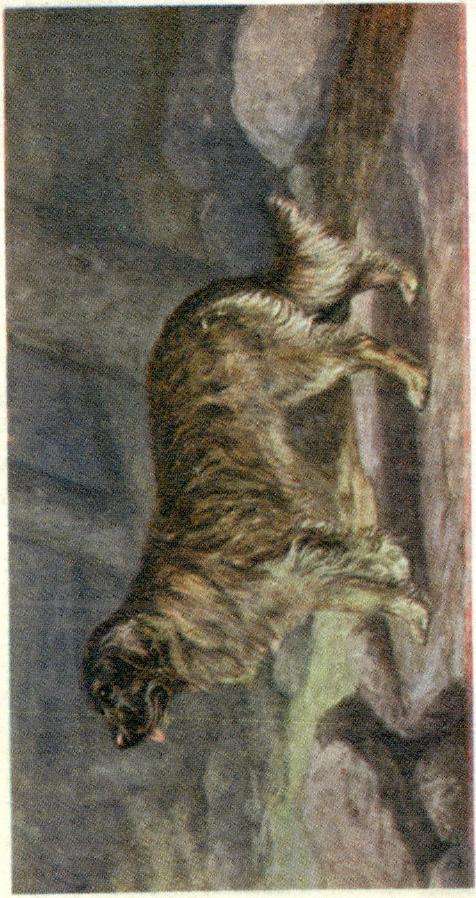

BLOODHOUND

Origin **Belgium**

The bloodhound is a beautiful dog. Its head is majestic, even if the supple, thin skin on its head and neck hangs down in deep folds. The forebears of these large, solemn and powerful hunting dogs lived in the Ardennes region of present-day Belgium about the year 1000. They were bred by the monks of the abbey of Saint-Hubert, and were known at the time as Saint-Hubert hounds. At the time, the nobles of the region used this hardy breed of scent hound on their hunting expeditions, because they could cover miles tracking large game without hesitation. The Saint-Hubert hound, which was then all black, later took on other colours: two-tone black and tan, liver and tan, and entirely red. It was taken to England with William the Conqueror in the eleventh century and took root in the island, where it received the name bloodhound. The breed would have died out in Europe in the nineteenth century if a group of British breeders had not reacted to this situation and reassembled breeding stock. The bloodhound today is used for its excellent sense of smell to find missing persons. It is a gently and sensitive dog. It has inherited a highly sociable nature from its ancestors. It may be reserved and sometimes stubborn, but it always obeys its master.

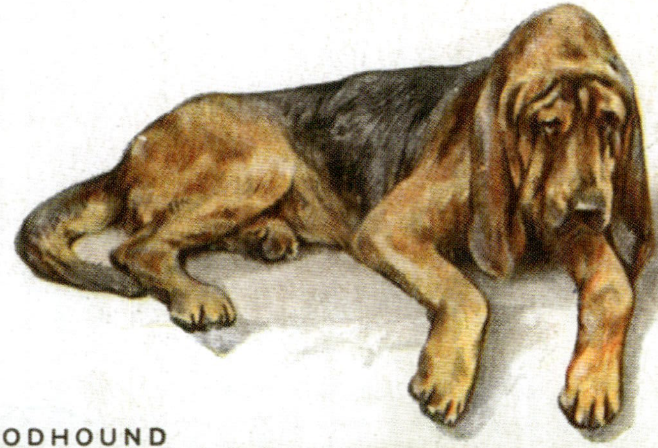

BLOODHOUND

XOLOITZCUINTLI

Origin **Mexico**

Hairless dogs are the work of nature, not of humans, who have played no part. Their being born that way is simply a matter of dominant genes. Hairless dogs are native to two countries in the Americas, Peru and Mexico, and their origins go back to the dawn of time. The Mexican hairless dog was given the name *xoloitzcuintli* because in the Aztec religion it symbolized the deity Xolotl, god of the sunset, twins and games. This pre-Colombian civilization also believed that it would guide souls on their long journey to underworld. The hairless dog has soft and smooth skin, the colouring of which varies from black and grey to blond, bronze, liver and a reddish tone. Its body is perfectly proportioned, with a large chest and long paws. It can have a few coarse hairs on its feet and paws. Some litters of puppies can be born with a coat of hair. These are not considered to be black sheep because they belong to a recognized variety, which the Mexicans call *itzcuintli*. The xoloitzcuintli is cheerful and intelligent. There are three sizes: standard, intermediate and miniature. Watchful, but never showing aggressive behaviour, this dog often hides from strangers.

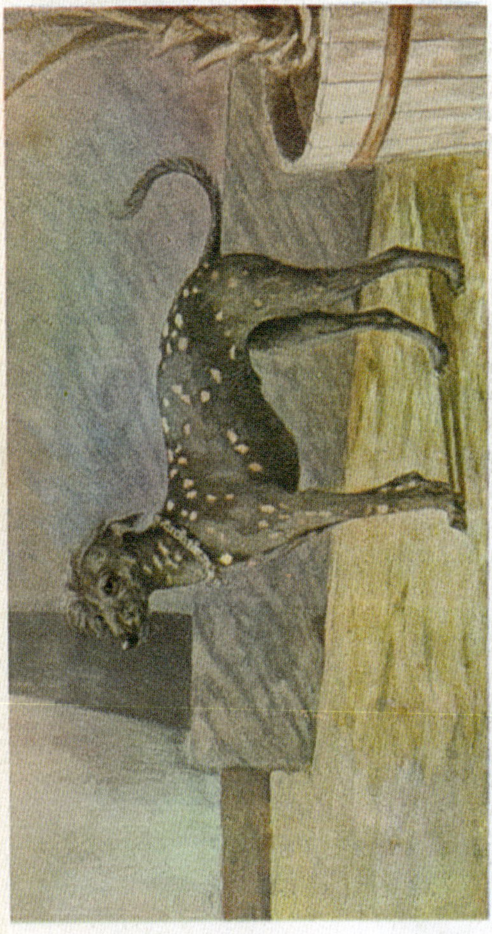

CHOW CHOW

Origin **China**

The chow chow, also known simply as the chow, made its first appearance in Europe at the court of Queen Victoria, who was given one as a gift in 1865. The animal had journeyed for thousands of miles from its home in China, where it had existed for more than 2,000 years. The Huns, Mongols and Tartars had used it as a guard dog, war dog and hunting dog. The chow chow first appeared in France in 1900, but it made few inroads because owning one remained the privilege of a few rich Parisians. It gradually gained the favour of breeders. The first breed club for chow chows was founded in 1926, before this dog found a definitive home in France. The chow chow is quite a striking dog. It has a lion-like silhouette, and it walks stiffly on paws resembling those of a cat. It has a proud bearing. Its expression seems to always be sullen, but this is not a feature of its temperament, only a physical trait. A bluish-black tongue hangs out of its partly opened mouth. Its lips and palate are also of the same colour. Its small and thick ears are slightly rounded at the tip. It has a strong body, with its tail set high and carried over the back. It is a tranquil, lively and agile dog. It is faithful, but it does not like great shows of affection. It is precisely this temperament that appeals to its master.

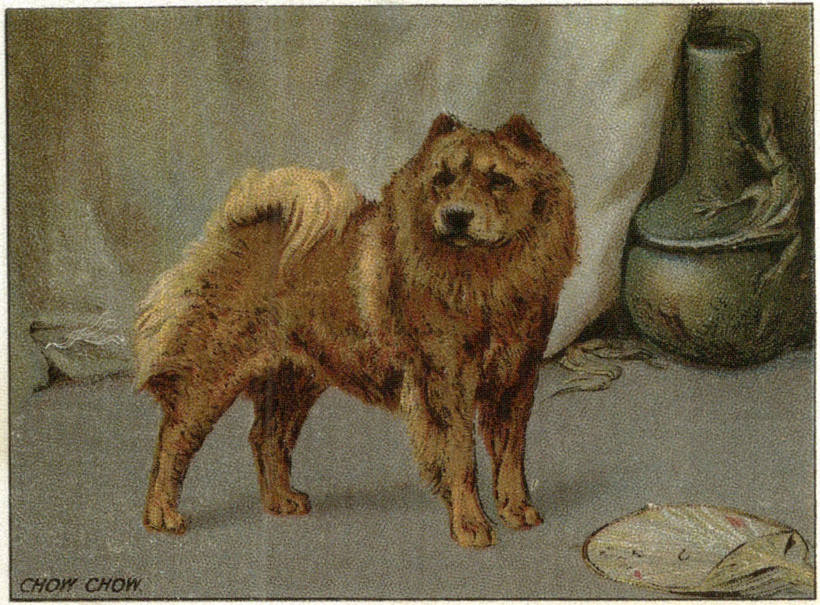
CHOW CHOW.

CLUMBER SPANIEL

Origin **Britain**

The origin of this dog is uncertain, but it is believed by some to have originated in France. It is even said that the French Duke of Noailles gave a few specimens to the Duke of Newcastle in the eighteenth century. This English aristocrat then took them to his estate of Clumber Park, after which the dog is named. The British were very soon drawn to the appearance of this dog, and they were bred as hunting dogs. They hunt silently, with an infallible sense of smell. The Clumber spaniel is relatively unknown in France. The Société Centrale Canine only recorded 19 dogs of this breed in its breed registry in 2010, compared to 5,214 cocker spaniels, for instance. In its official birthplace of Britain, the breed is just as unknown; between 160–220 births are recorded each year. However, this dog has great qualities. The Clumber spaniel has been called the 'aristocrat of the spaniels' because of its graceful physique. It has abundant, close, silky and straight hair, with feathering on its chest and legs. It coat is all white, with lemon or orange markings. It muzzle is also freckled. The Clumber spaniel is the strongest of the spaniels. It has a heavy set frame with short legs and measures about 45 centimetres. Its gentleness and docile nature make it quite endearing to families, in towns and in the country.

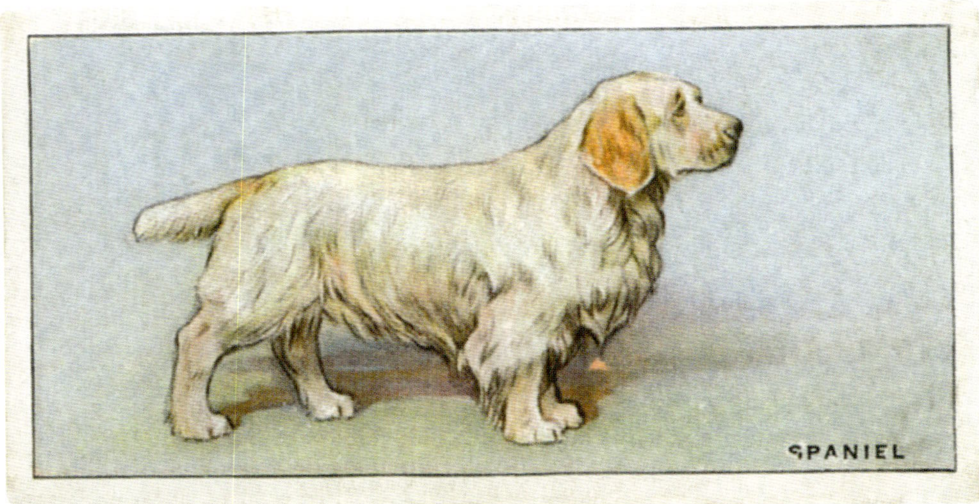
SPANIEL

ENGLISH COCKER SPANIEL

Origin **Britain**

The brown eyes of certain cocker spaniels look so melancholy that the French dedicated an expression to them, regard de cocker, which means a sad look. However, behind this perceived sadness is great tenderness. The cocker spaniel is filled with love and affection for the people with whom it lives. Its hair is as light and fine as silk. Its coat can be black, fawn, brown, white with ticking, or tricolour. Its body and legs are well feathered, as is its tail, if it has not been docked. The modestly sized cocker spaniel is an active, exuberant and playful dog. It is able to participate in all human activities, including naps and long walks, where it loves to use up its boundless energy. The cocker spaniel is constantly on the lookout for quarry, because it has not always been a companion dog. Its forebears were actually hunting dogs, mainly of woodcock - in fact, its name, cocker, is derived from this bird. The cocker spaniel has been recognized in Britain since 1892. The French Spaniel Club was founded six years later. France soon became infatuated with the qualities of this dog, both for its company and hunting prowess. The English cocker spaniel has an American cousin, the smaller American cocker spaniel.

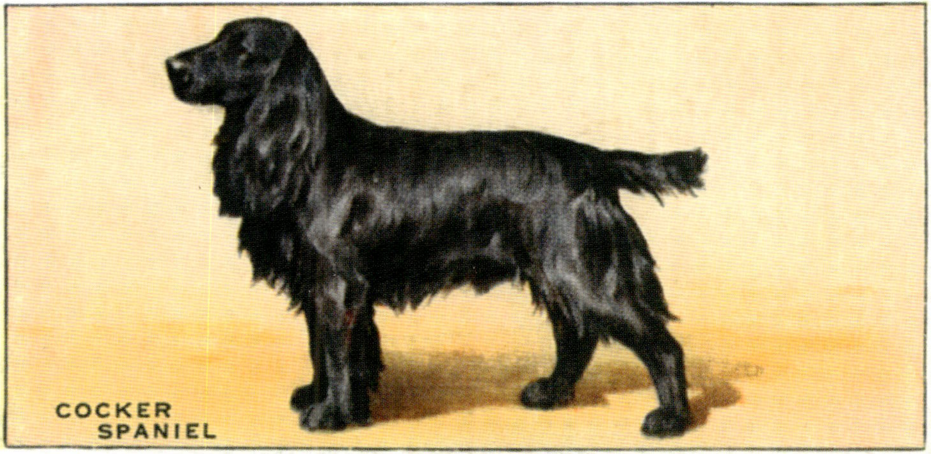
COCKER
SPANIEL

ROUGH COLLIE

Origin **Britain**

The collie, also known as the Scotch shepherd, originated in Scotland. There is no doubt that it was the result of crossing local breeds with dogs brought by the Romans when they invaded the British Isles in 55 BC. They were long used to herd sheep. In the nineteenth century, when the first dog shows were held in Britain, dog breeders showed interest in the breed. By selective breeding, they improved the dog's appearance, which they made more elegant, and they gradually began to set the breed standard. The results were so appealing that the collie joined the court of Queen Victoria. It also gained popularity in France, where a collie breed club was founded in 1912. Lovers of the dog are charmed by its friendly nature, intelligent look and proud appearance. Its dense coat can vary in colouring between sable, sable and white, tricolour, and blue merle mottling. In the 1950s, its loyalty and bravery were highlighted through television, when a collie named Lassie became the face of the television series of the same name. The rough collie has a less known, short-haired cousin, the smooth collie, which is used to assist sight-impaired and disabled people. Both varieties love family life.

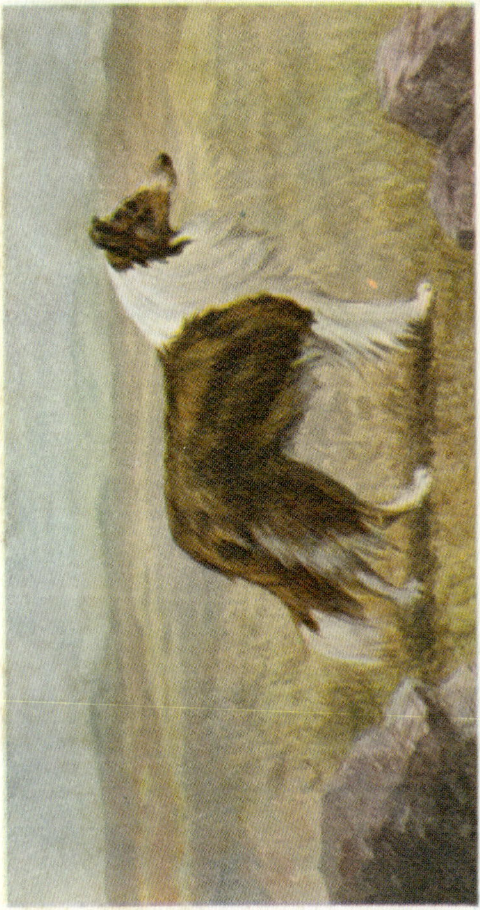

MONGREL

Origin **Earth**

The mongrel, or mutt, is the only dog to have escaped human control. No selective breeding has shaped its silhouette. The fruit of random encounters between total stranger mothers and fathers, the mongrel can be proud to be the offspring of an ancient line, perhaps the oldest of all dog lines. It was conceived on the corner of a street, hence its French name *corniaud*, which comes from the word *corne*, which in the seventeenth century had the meaning of 'corner'. Mother nature chiselled its body and forged its temperament. The mongrel was adapted to its environment and the quarry it was able to catch. More often, it finds its food in what humans throw away. The mongrel of the south does not resemble the mongrel of the north, the Asian mongrel or the American mongrel. In India, and later in Asia, it is called the pariah dog, whose colouring is often sandy or yellow. The mongrel is often the outcast of the canine world. It is a street dog, and knows the law of the street. It has managed to survive there. Humans have praised its bravery and intelligence, but have also accused it of spreading rabies.

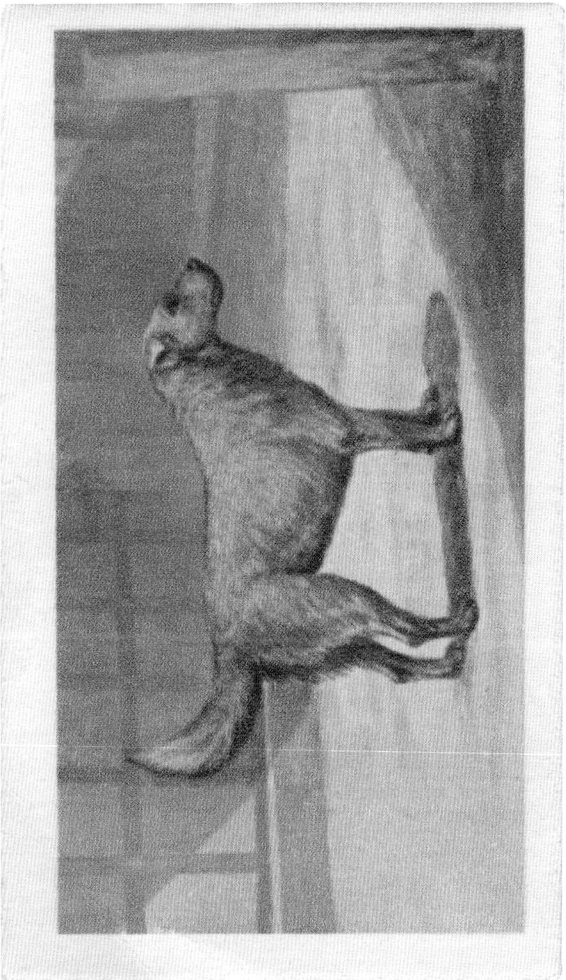

DALMATIAN
Origin **Croatia**

The elegance of the Dalmatian has long concealed its tried-and-tested endurance. This dog, with its black or liver-spotted white coat, once ran for miles beside horses in the eighteenth century. It escorted the most varied teams on the roads of Britain, first mail coaches, and then the carriages of the aristocracy. It was known as a carriage dog at the time. Its role? To protect travellers from bandits during the day, and the horses and coachman at night. In Britain and the United States, it also ran ahead of horse-drawn fire engines. When it was not out on a mission, it would guard the fire station. While the breed standard was recognized by the British in 1890, its origins remain a little controversial. However, the Fédération Cynophile Internationale (World Canine Organization) recognized Croatia – Dalmatia, in particular – as its country of origin, because this dog appeared in different writings and paintings in this region during the seventeenth and eighteenth centuries. Honest, sensitive and faithful, the Dalmatian is an affectionate and sometimes independent dog with a great need to burn off energy.

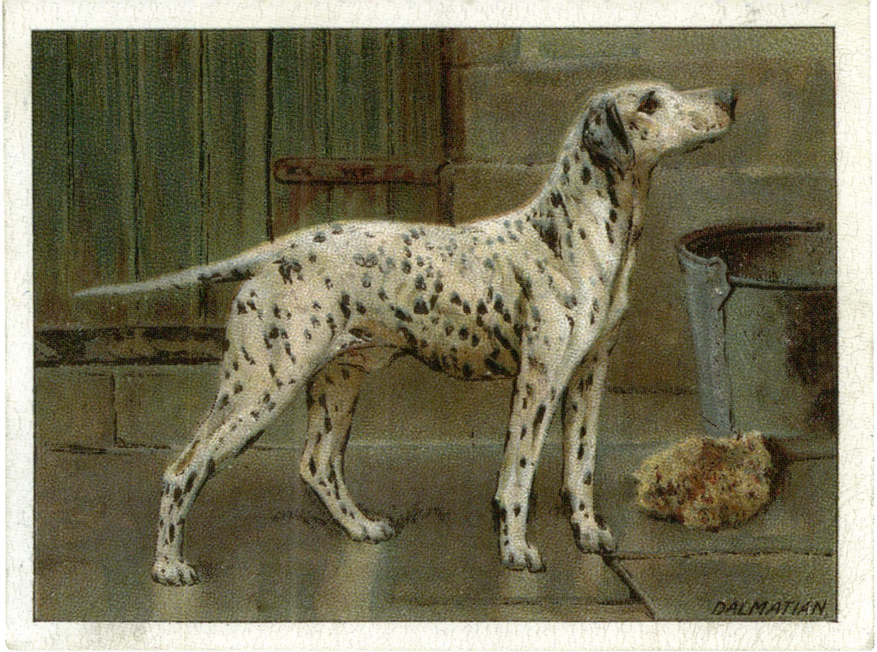
DALMATIAN.

DANDIE DINMONT TERRIER

Origin **Britain**

Despite its short and stocky appearance, the Dandie Dinmont terrier is not descended from the basset hound; it is a pure-bred terrier. To create this breed, a Scottish farmer in the seventeenth century crossed an old breed of Scottish terrier with a Bedlington terrier and an otterhound. Nobody knows what it was called at that time. Two centuries later, it was given the name of a character from Sir Walter Scott's novel *Guy Mannering* (1815), who owned six terriers. The dogs belonging to this farmer were all named Pepper or Mustard, depending on the colour of their coat. Interestingly, the two coat colours recognized for the Dandie Dinmont terrier are mustard (reddish-brown to light fawn) and pepper (black to silvery grey); Sir Walter Scott may have something to do with this... The breed was officially recognized in Britain in 1876. Today, this small terrier, which weighs 8–11 kilograms, no longer hunts as such. It has become rare, even in its homeland, to the point where it is classified as a vulnerable breed. However, the Dandie Dinmont terrier has a sweet little face that will upstage any of his terrier cousins. This dog is bursting with life, intelligent, affectionate and sensitive, sometimes stubborn, and independent. Like all self-respecting terriers, it takes to family life with great relish.

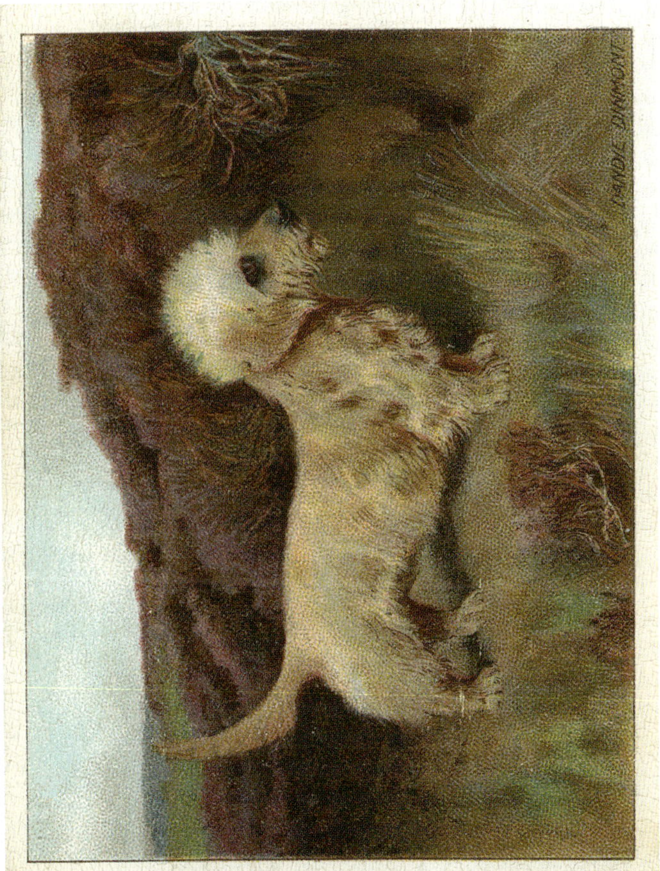

DOBERMANN

Origin **Germany**

This breed owes everything to Friedrich Louis Dobermann (1834–94), a man who occupied himself with several professions in the small town of Apolda, in the Thuringia region. He was a tax collector, stray dog catcher and an amateur dog breeder. As a tax collector, he sometimes faced the animosity of his fellow citizens and often had to carry large sums of money. This led him to the idea of creating a dog breed that was perfectly suited to his needs. He did not hesitate to take dogs from the dog pound, where he chose so-called 'butcher's dogs' to achieve his goal. Dobermann crossed them with the black and tan sheepdogs of the region, and then with pinschers, German mastiffs and Beaucerons, sheepdogs from the Beauce region of France. He finally created his desired dog in about 1870. It was smaller and squatter than the breed we know today. Otto Goeller, who continued the selective breeding process, turned the Dobermann into a muscular, lively and elegant dog. This strong-natured dog is friendly and peaceful. While it remains an excellent guard dog, it also makes a very good pet.

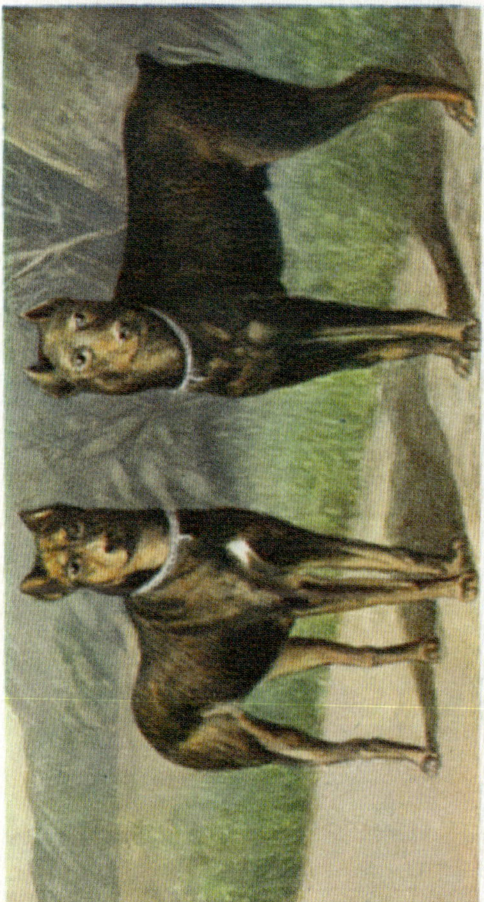

GREAT DANE

Origin **Germany**

The closest ancestor to this German (despite its name) mastiff-like dog is the Bullenbeisser ('bulldog'). This now-extinct breed once baited bulls as a sport for humans. It was crossed with the alaunt gentile, a Molossian dog used to hunt large game animals in the Middle Ages. From this cross-breeding came the Ulmer dogge, English dogge and Danish dogge, among others, each with a different size and coat. In 1878, a committee formed by seven breeders and judges decided to combine all these types into a single breed, the Deutsche Dogge, or Great Dane as it is known in English. Because of its great beauty, it is referred to as the 'Apollo of dogs', a title that has never been usurped. This athletic dog has a statuesque appearance; its silhouette is large, powerful and harmonious. Its very short hair is dense and smooth, and gleams in the light. The long, lean and muscular neck proudly bears a magnificent, finely chiselled head. The Great Dane's large size is very imposing: males measure at least 80 centimetres at the withers, while females reach 72 centimetres. This breed is good-hearted. It is friendly and very attached to its family, but shows reserve towards strangers.

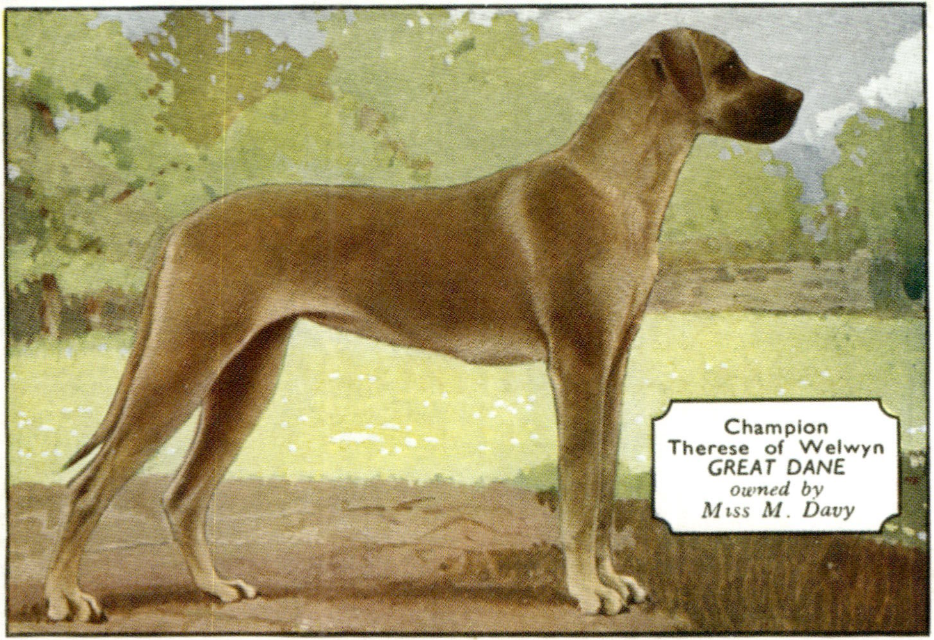
Champion
Therese of Welwyn
GREAT DANE
owned by
Miss M. Davy

DOGUE DE BORDEAUX

Origin **France**

This dog has a distant ancestor in the alaunt veantre, a medieval hunting dog. The Count of Foix, Gaston Phébus, described in his fourteenth-century *Livre de la Chasse* (Hunting Book) that an individual of this breed 'had a bite that was stronger than that of three greyhounds. The history of the dogue de Bordeaux only became certain in the nineteenth century. At the time, the breed was only known in the Aquitaine region of France. Like its assumed ancestor, it was used to hunt wild boar. It was sometimes used for fighting and for protecting property and livestock. In 1863, eight dogues de Bordeaux were presented at the first dog show in Paris, held at the Jardin d'Acclimatation. Three types of dogues, mastiff-like dogs, existed at the time, the Parisian, Toulousain and Bordelais dogues. The dogue de Bordeaux was in danger of dying out in the nineteenth century, had it not been for the interest of enthusiasts in saving them. They were brought back from the brink, and the first breed standard appeared in 1896. The breed was later developed to have a muscular and harmonious body. Its short fawn coat is soft to the touch. The dogue de Bordeaux is a good guardian, and is calm and patient, preferring to sit beside its master than live alone in the most beautiful of gardens.

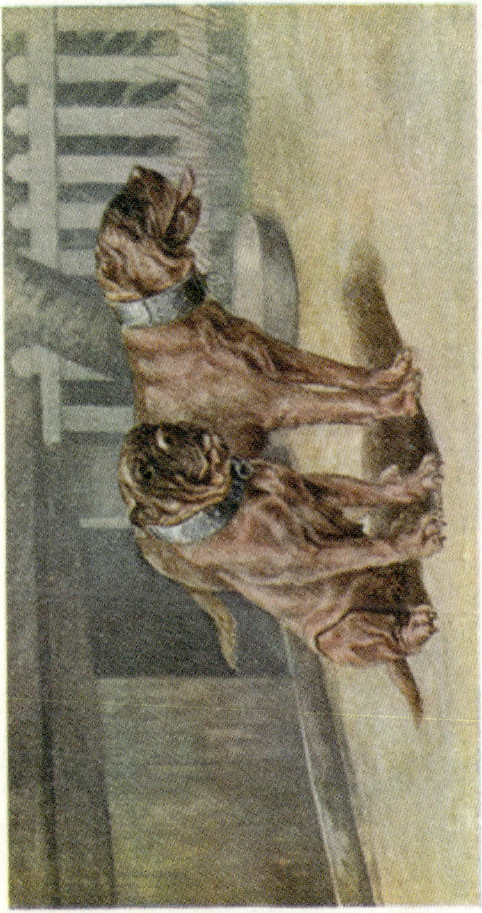

ENGLISH SPRINGER SPANIEL

Origin **Britain**

It was only in 1900 that the British springer spaniel received its definitive name; until then it was known as the Norfolk spaniel. Like most spaniels, this dog probably originated in Spain, from where it spread all over Europe. The springer spaniel has a characteristically happy disposition. This cheerful and friendly dog loves to please all the members of its family, children and parents alike. While it is kept as a companion pet by many, it is also an excellent hunting dog. In the Middle Ages, it actually provided assistance to hunters using nets, falcons, traps, and even greyhounds. The springer's role was to find, or 'spring', the quarry and drive it towards the trap set by the hunter. It could move over any terrain, and met no resistance in the undergrowth or in marshes. Its close and straight coat could withstand the harshest weather conditions. Because it is extremely docile and has a keen sense of smell, the springer spaniel is sometimes used today to detect explosives and drugs. Its liver-and-white or black-and-white coat feathers its ears, legs and body. The English springer spaniel is the largest of the British spaniels used for hunting on plains and in woodland, measuring about 51 centimetres at the withers. It has one guilty pleasure: food.

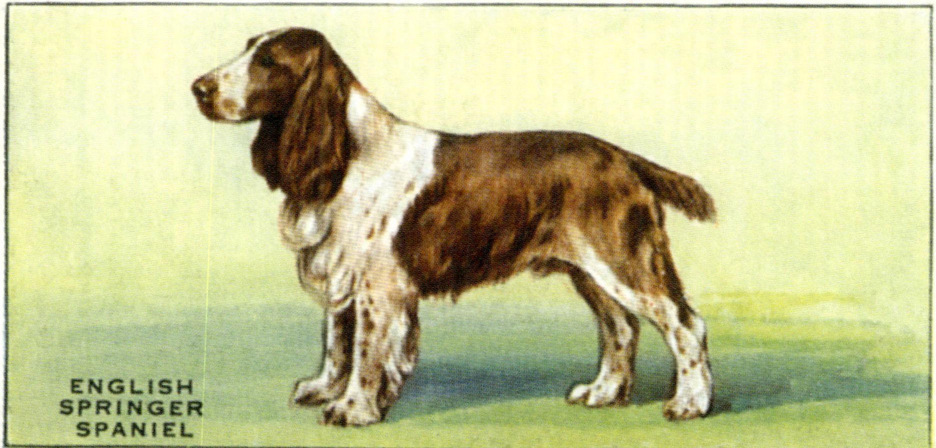
ENGLISH
SPRINGER
SPANIEL

JAPANESE CHIN

Origin **Japan**

In the year 732, the ancestor of the Japanese chin was a gift to strengthen diplomatic ties between the kings of Korea and the emperor of Japan. The animal may not have served as the cornerstone for negotiations, but it succeeded in quickly conquering the hearts of the Japanese with its silky, black-and-white or fawn-and-white coat and its round black eyes. It was known as the chin in Japan, and a large number of them were imported. The animal even became an imperial dog. During the reign of Shogun Tokugawa Tsunayoshi (1680–1709), it was bred at his castle in Edo, modern-day Tokyo, as a lapdog. In the seventeenth century, the English buccaneer Searles took a few specimens back to the English court. King Charles II of England, a lover of miniature dog breeds, also adopted the lightweight breed; the Japanese chin weighs less than 6 kilograms. In the course of the following centuries, this little dog became one of the darlings of European high society. The Impressionist Manet, in 1875, and Renoir, a year later, painted their pretty little faces. This dog has as proud silhouette and a long, abundant, straight coat. Despite its small size, this is not a delicate dog. It is robust, sensitive and affectionate.

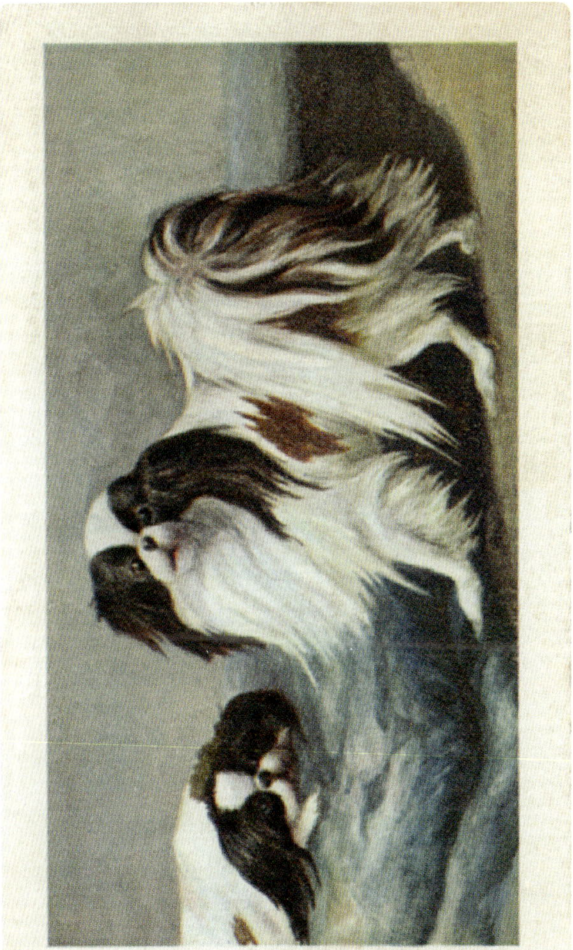

KING CHARLES SPANIEL

Origin **Britain**

Miniature dogs found favour in the royal courts of Europe the fifteenth century. King Charles II of England showed even more enthusiasm than his forefathers by lending his name to this pocket-sized spaniel. He owned a large number of them and they even escorted him to his chamber, a great privilege considering that their hunting relatives would have to remain in their kennels. To achieve a breed of such reduced size, there is no doubt that selection involved the smallest setter dogs. They may even have been crossed with Japanese chins or other Asian breeds. Snub-nosed dogs became fashionable in the seventeenth century, and enthusiasts of the King Charles Spaniel endeavoured to give their favourite dog this appearance. The King Charles spaniel is a lightweight dog, weighing 3.6–6.3 kilograms. It is even lighter than its cousin, the Cavalier King Charles spaniel, which weighs 5.4-8 kilograms. This dog has an elegant and compact silhouette and long, straight and silky hair. Its coat can be coloured black and tan, tricolour (black, white and tan) Blenheim (white with chestnut red patches) or ruby (rich chestnut red). Intelligent, reserved, gentle and affectionate, the King Charles spaniel is a devoted companion.

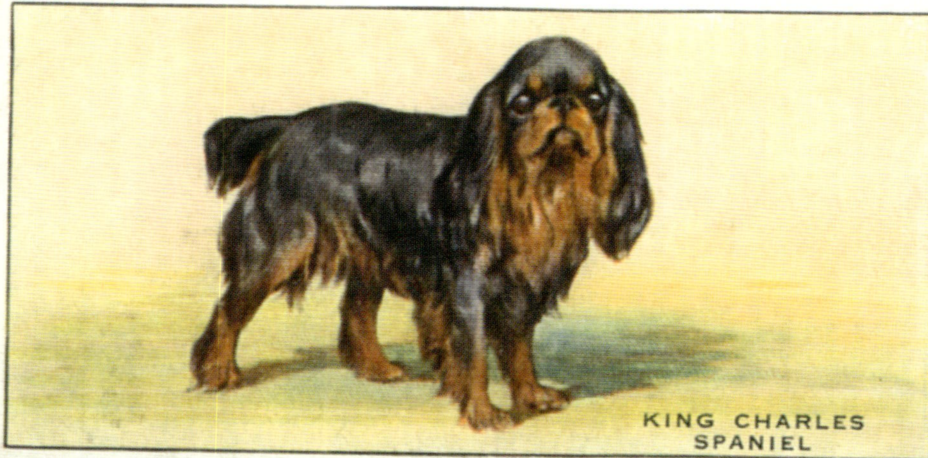
KING CHARLES
SPANIEL

PEKINGESE

Origin **China**

The Pekingese is an inexhaustible source of legends in China. According to one such legend, a lion fell madly in love with a marmoset. Because their love was impossible, the king of beasts appealed to Buddha so that he could take the size of his beloved marmoset. The fruit of their legendary union would be the Pekingese, sometimes nicknamed the 'lion dog'. The Pekingese is above all a dog of emperors. For centuries it graced the halls of the Chinese imperial court, throughout the entire succession of dynasties in Peking (modern-day Beijing). The British encountered the breed during their siege of the Chinese capital. They discovered five specimens in the Summer Palace, which were sent back to Britain and offered to Queen Victoria, who named hers Looty; to the Duchess of Wellington; and the Duchess of Richmond, who created the first English strain, the Goodwoods. Despite its squat silhouette, the Pekingese is very dignified. It has abundant, long and flat hair, which forms a mane around its head. It is faithful, although sometimes aloof, but it shows no fear or aggressiveness. Its dark, round eyes gleam with intelligence and liveliness.

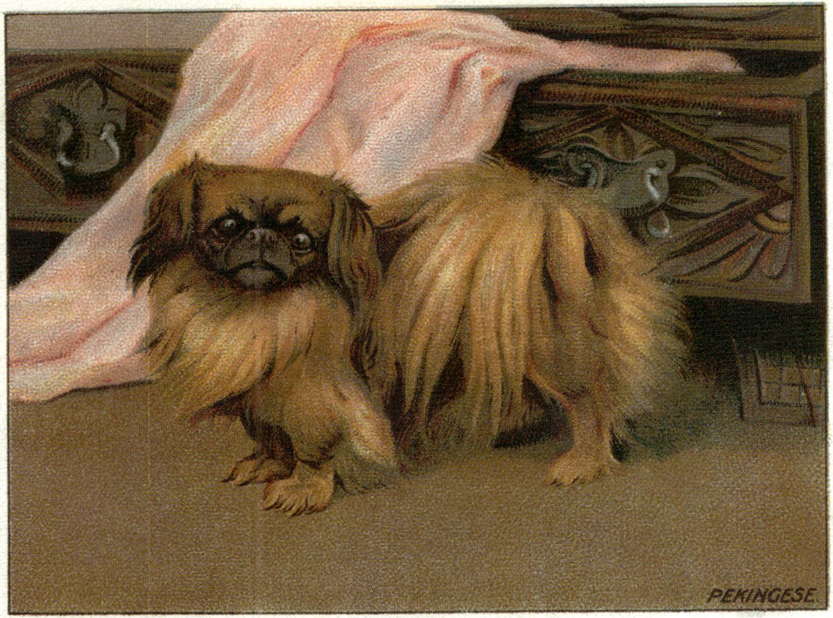
PEKINGESE.

CANADIAN ESKIMO
Origin **Canada**

For centuries, if not millennia, Canadian Eskimo dogs have served the Inuit people in the harsh Canadian Arctic region as a drafting dog, hunting dog and pack animal. Hitched to a sledge, it could travel for miles pulling loads of 45–80 kilograms. It would hunt for seals beside its master. It would also track and then hold off a musk ox or polar bear while waiting for the hunters to arrive. It became a pack animal in summer, hauling loads as heavy as 15 kilograms on its back. Like other primitive dogs, the Canadian Eskimo dog would eat seal, caribou, fish and walrus. However, the modernization of Inuit society has practically led to its extinction. In 1976, the Canadian Eskimo Dog Research Foundation in the Northwest Territories began an attempt to preserve the breed by bringing together a few individuals acquired on the Boothia and Melville Peninsulas, as well as on Baffin Island. The breeding programme the foundation then established managed to save from extinction this hard-working dog, which is able to withstand the cold of the far north. Canada later officially recognized the standard for the breed, which has thick and straight ears and a thick tail. The Canadian Eskimo dog is gentle and affectionate with people. It reacts quickly to stimuli, and makes a better companion for adults than for children. On 1 May 2000, it became the symbol for Canada's Nunavut territory.

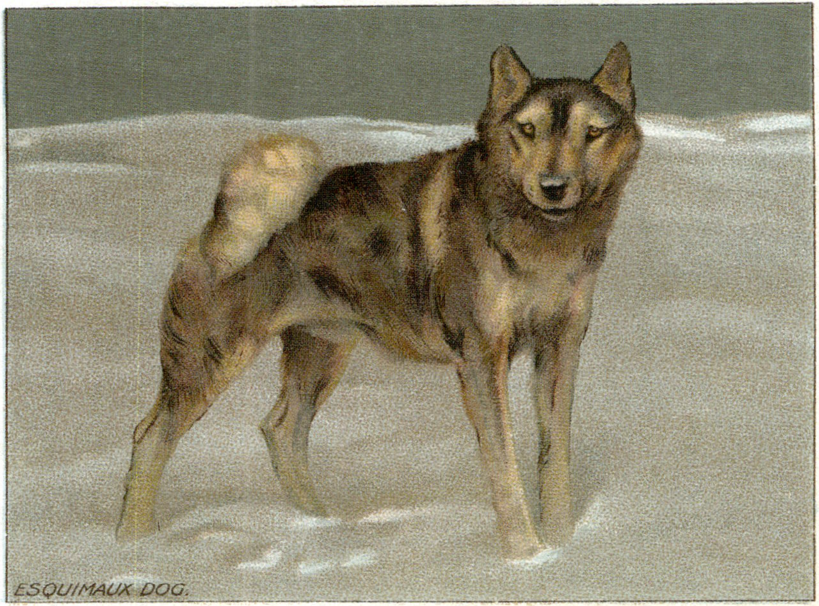
ESQUIMAUX DOG.

ENGLISH FOXHOUND

Origin **Britain**

The baying of the hounds has long resounded through the English countryside. Since the early seventeenth century, this dog has been kept in packs trained mainly to hunt foxes, and to track down deer and hares. In each region of the island of Great Britain, humans have shaped this breed in the image of the local landscape. There are now five varieties of foxhound in Britain, one of which is the English foxhound. However, they share their features: hazel eyes, a keen expression, and a short, dense coat in all colours. The Masters of Foxhounds Association have been in charge of the breed register for this breed since the eighteenth century. There are currently 188 packs registered in Britain. Since the enactment of a law banning fox hunting and hare coursing in 2004, foxhounds mainly chase lures. This strong and muscular dog is friendly with people, but is rarely found outside of its pack as a family pet.

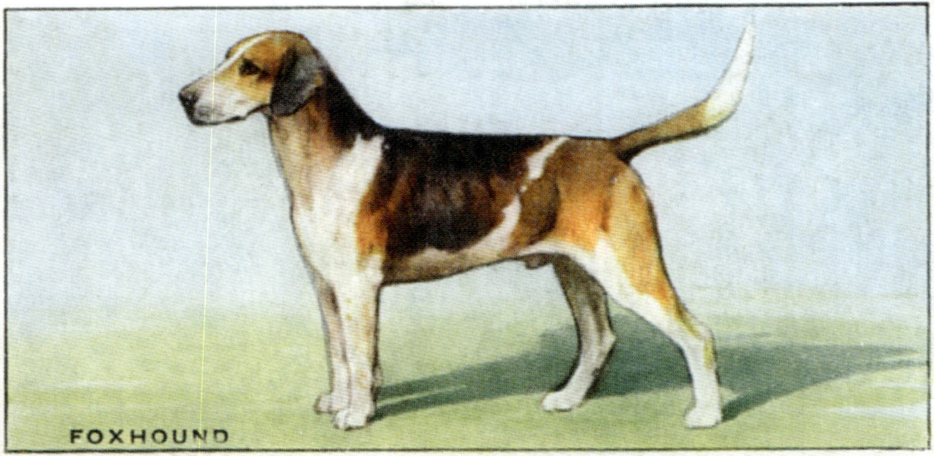
FOXHOUND

WIRE FOX TERRIER

Origin **Britain**

The fox terrier appeared in the nineteenth century. It was created at the time particularly to take part in one of the popular British pastimes of the period: the fox hunt. Because of its modest size (less than 40 centimetres at the withers), this dog can sneak into even the smallest of dens to flush out the animal. This specialization gave the fox terrier its name. However, no record has been kept of the cross-breeding through which it was created. Beagles and other British terriers have been suggested. Whatever the case, since this dog was created there have been two types, the wire fox terrier and the smooth fox terrier. The Fox Terrier Club was founded in 1876 for this breed, and the standards for the two varieties were written up in the same year. During the twentieth century, the wire fox terrier moved from hunting grounds and into high society. It is true that its kind and sociable temperament towards people have made it much loved. The friendly and faithful character of Snowy, from the Adventures of Tintin comic series, is an illustration of this. Even though it is not a hunter today, the wire fox terrier retains the energy and fearlessness of its forebears.

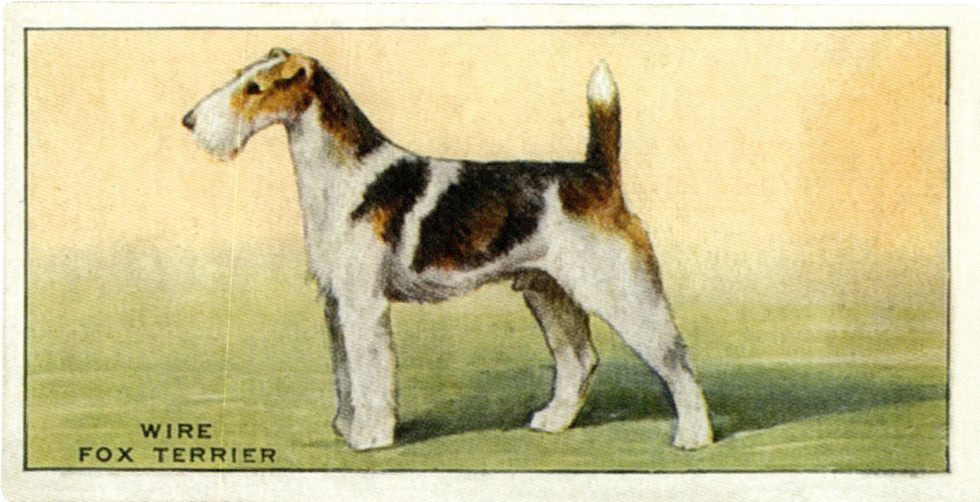
WIRE
FOX TERRIER

SMOOTH FOX TERRIER

Origin **Britain**

This dog was created in Britain in the nineteenth century especially for fox hunting. The aim was to produce a fearless and resilient dog to chase a fox right to its den. This particular talent was what gave this medium-sized dog, weighing 7–9 kilograms, its name. To give it an elegant but sturdy appearance, the British resorted to cross-breeding between beagles and other terrier breeds. Not all fox terriers are alike: some are wire fox terriers and others are smooth fox terriers. The two breeds were distinguished in 1876, when their breed standards were established. In the early twentieth century, the smooth fox terrier became popular with the general public in France, undoubtedly because of the success of the comic *Ric et Rac* by Pol Rab, which appeared in the 1920s. However, in the period after the First World War, its wire-haired counterpart succeeded in winning over the hearts of families. Could the famous Snowy, closely resembling a wire fox terrier, have had something to do with this? Today, the smooth fox terrier is as charming as its cousin, with its pure white coat or white coat with black, fawn or tan markings. It is also brave, tenacious and lively, qualities it has inherited from its ancestors. With this temperament, it does not always accept other animals sharing its home, but it has unwavering affection for its masters.

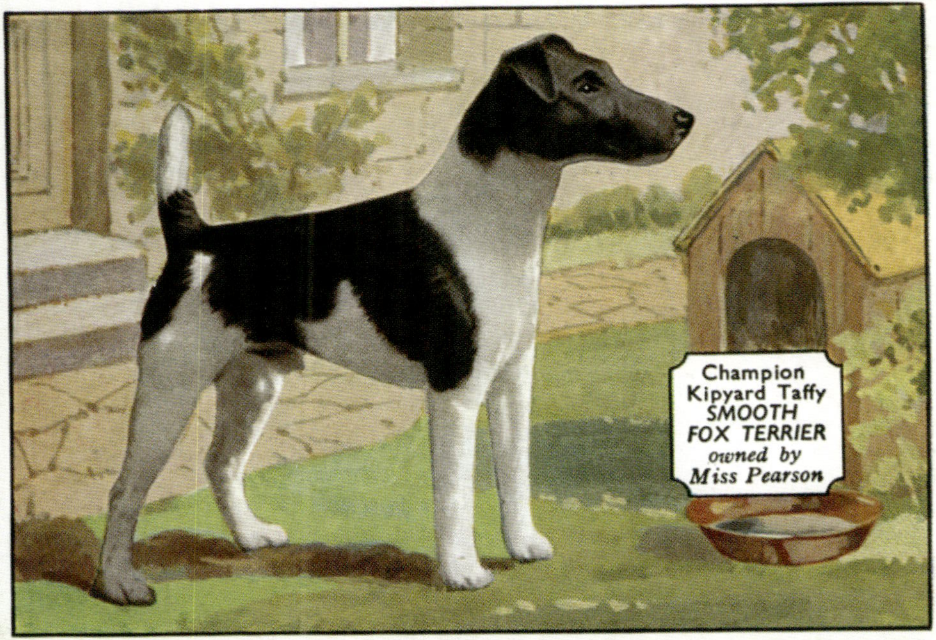
Champion
Kipyard Taffy
SMOOTH
FOX TERRIER
owned by
Miss Pearson

FRENCH HOUND

Origin **France**

There are three versions of the French hound: the French tricolour hound, the French black-and-white hound, and the French white-and-orange hound. All three are hunting dogs; all three have short hair; and all three were given an official breed standard quite late, in 1957. Their ancestors were ancient strains of French and English scenthounds. The French tricolour hound is the result of crosses between the large Anglo-French tricolour hound, the Poitevin and the Billy. The French black-and-white hound has a distant ancestor in the Saintogne dog, although its current silhouette appeared in the 1850s as the result of cross-breeding between Poitevins and Gascon Saintongeois. The origins of the French white-and-orange hound are more obscure. Some suggest the Billy, but nothing is less certain. Today, these three dogs quite often belong to hunting packs. The packs chase deer, roe deer and wild boar. The expression of their dark eyes shines with intelligence. Gentle and friendly with people, they make good life-long companions, as long as they can burn off their energy. However, despite all these qualities, the French hound remains quite rare in France.

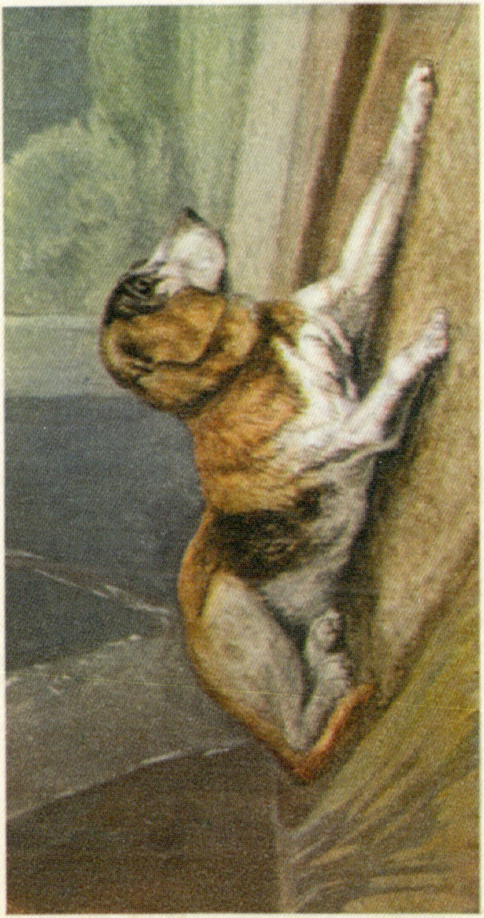

GOLDEN RETRIEVER

Origin **Britain**

People have become so enamoured of this breed that today it is now ahead of the labrador in the French LOF breed register. The friendly temperament of the golden retriever has given it an excellent reputation, but before becoming a steadfast companion for families, the golden retriever was a hunting dog, famed for retrieving quarry for its master without leaving as much as a bite mark. It is used today for detecting explosives or as an assistance dog for the disabled. Novices often call it as a long-haired labrador. This confusion can be explained by their common ancestor, the Saint John's water dog, which used to help Canadian fishermen pull their nets onto their boats in the seventeenth century. But the golden retriever originated in Britain, where Lord Tewdmonth began the selective breeding process by crossing wavy-coated retrievers with now-extinct Tweed water spaniels. In short, the golden retriever is a sociable but rustic, sensitive but energetic dog - and one that will never leave its master.

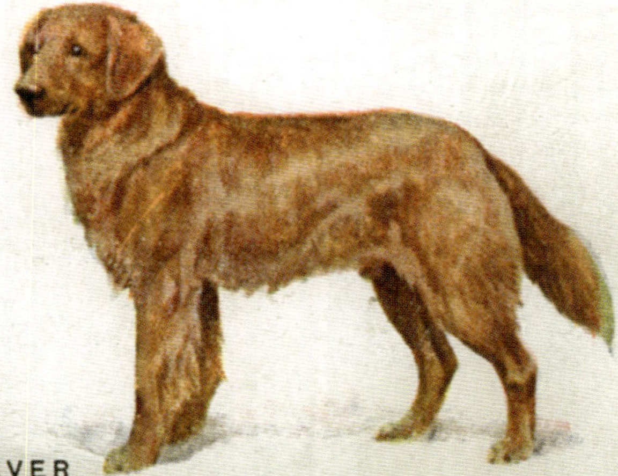

GOLDEN
RETRIEVER

GREYHOUND

Origin **Britain**

Only a cheetah could beat the elegant greyhound in a race. This swift sighthound can actually reach speeds of 70 kilometres per hour. It has the physique of an athlete and a long and robust silhouette – a male can reach a height of 71–76 centimetres. Its legs are muscular, its head fine and elongated, and its neck is supple and arched. In order to keep fit, it has to train constantly at a fast pace for a distance of 4–8 kilometres each day. Although the breed was created in Britain, the greyhound may have roots in ancient Egypt, although the Greeks were the first to initiate its ancestors in racing. When the British set out the rules of coursing in 1750, the animal was ready to take part in all races. The greyhound at the time was a lighter breed than the one that races on modern-day greyhound tracks. And there was no such thing as chasing a lure, like it does today, because only a hare would make it run against other dogs. Today, the greyhound cannot always resist the temptation to chase a cat or another small animal... but it is calm inside the home, sometimes reserved, and completely devoted to its master.

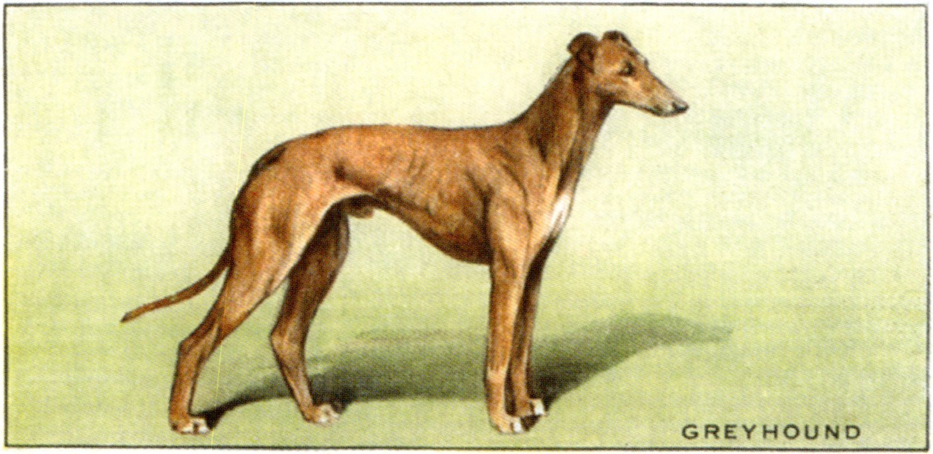
GREYHOUND

GRIFFON NIVERNAIS

Origin **France**

The shaggy and robust griffon Nivernais is a dog with strong ties to the Nivernais region of France. Its ancestors were Gallic hounds and grey Saint Louis dogs. The former accompanied the Segusiavi, a Celtic tribe of Gaul, from what is now the Lyon and Le Forez regions of modern France. The latter would have been brought back from Palestine by King Louis IX of France, later Saint Louis, during the Crusades. This grey dog was long the favourite for French royal packs until King Francis I preferred white greffier (clerk's) dogs, which would later be known as the king's white hounds. Somehow, it managed to survive in the Nivernais. In the nineteenth century, enthusiasts wanted to revive its breeding and found a few local dogs with which to make this possible. No doubt, by crossing them with the griffons de Bresse, they created the griffon Nivernais. In the early twentieth century, a little griffon Vendéen, fox hound and otterhound blood was added to this dog to improve the breed. The griffon Nivernais today is a pack dog of modest size. Normally calm and obedient, it can become stubborn and independent when tracking game. Its qualities are prized mainly when hunting wild boar. The hair at the edge of its coat is much darker than that of the base, and its coat always has a black overlay. Its hair is long and bushy, coarse and quite strong, which is suited to the high grass and thickets that it loves to cross.

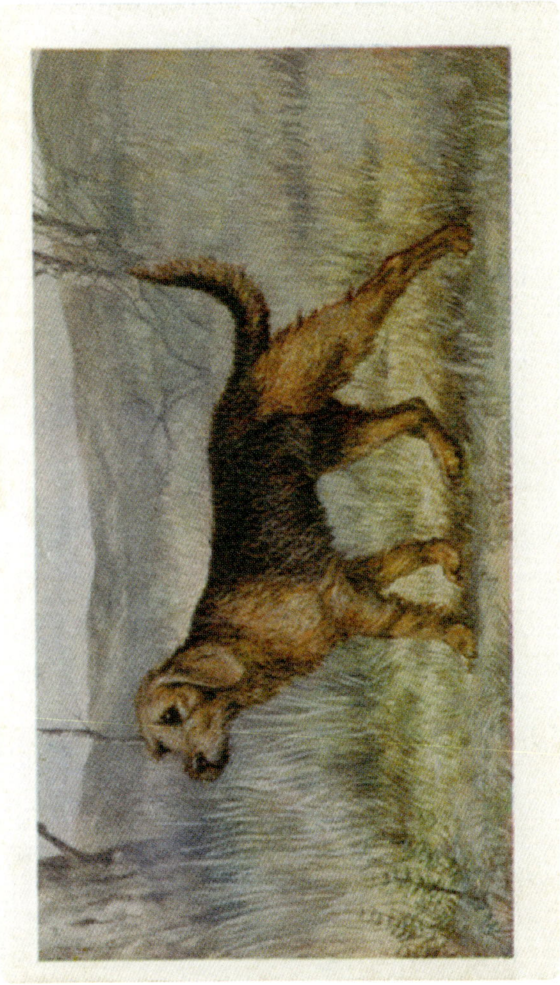

LAIKA

Origin **Russia**

The laika, whose name in Russian means 'barker', is a family of dogs resembling the spitz. There are three main variants: the East-Siberian laika, the West-Siberian laika, and the Russian-European laika. The Fédération Cynophile Internationale (World Canine Organization) recognizes the three breeds and has established their respective breed standards. Laikas are working dogs bred from dogs native to northern Russia and Siberia. They would follow hunters on their quest for game. The three laikas have a well-developed sense of smell and were sometimes used to pull sledges. The hair on their necks forms a thick and attractive collar. Their coat consists of coarse and straight hair, with a soft, abundant and woolly undercoat that allows them to withstand the icy temperatures of their home regions. Their tail is tightly curled up over their back. All three breeds make lively and balanced companions. The East-Siberian laika is undoubtedly the calmest of the three. Its coat can have a black-and-tan, black, black-and-white, or black colouring. Its qualities are mainly put to use for hunting large game. It resembles the smaller Russian-European laika. Their West-Siberian cousin is white, salt and pepper, red or grey. Hunters appreciate it for its ability to track down a single game animal, the highly prized marten.

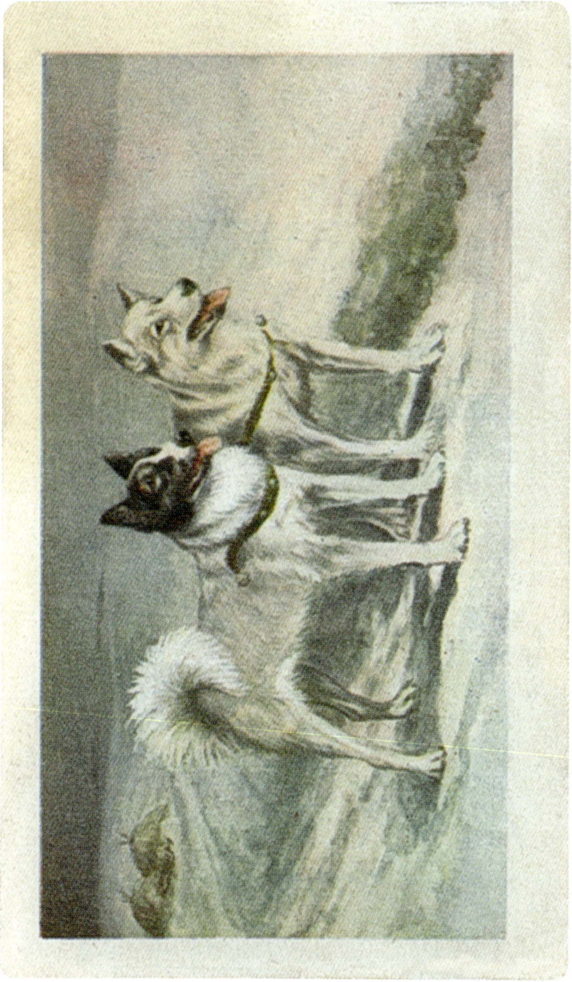

DEERHOUND

Origin **Britain**

This dog was already found in Scotland before the arrival of the Romans in the British Isles in 55 BC. The ancestor of this breed would have been the vertragu, a sighthound of Asian origin that arrived in the wake of Phoenician merchants. The deerhound has a different appearance to that of its cousin the greyhound. It has a thick, close-lying coat with coarse and ragged hair that is crisp to the touch, but under its shaggy coat are the same qualities developed by the other large sighthounds. This dog is actually as fast and hardy as any other. Its strength has led it to track down large quarry. The Scots would use it for deer hunts in the Highlands, until the rise of shooting and deforestation at the end of the nineteenth century led them to use other breeds. Today, even though it almost never hunts, the deerhound has not lost its qualities of speed and endurance, which is why it is entered into racing and coursing events together with greyhounds. The gentle and friendly deerhound makes a good companion.

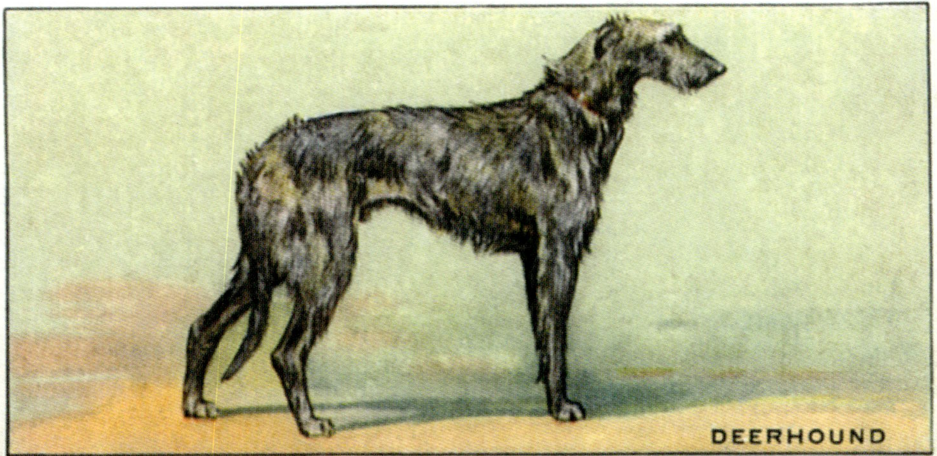
DEERHOUND

MANCHESTER TERRIER

Origin **Britain**

In the early nineteenth century, the inhabitants of English industrial towns used terrier-like dogs to kill rats. Rat-baiting became a popular sport and combats between dogs and rodents were held. It was with this purpose in mind that terriers were crossed with whippets, creating a dog with the aggressiveness of the former and the lightness of the latter. The result was the Manchester terrier. As its name indicates, the cradle of this breed was the large industrial city of Manchester in the north of England. The elegance and sturdiness of this new dog was appealing, and it soon became successful. Its coat is dense, smooth, short and glossy; its eyes are dark and bright; and its small V-shaped ears, previously cropped, hang close to its head. These features give it a mischievous look. Its colouring is jet black and a rich mahogany tan. This faithful dog has a cheerful and alert temperament, and makes a good pet in both city and country.

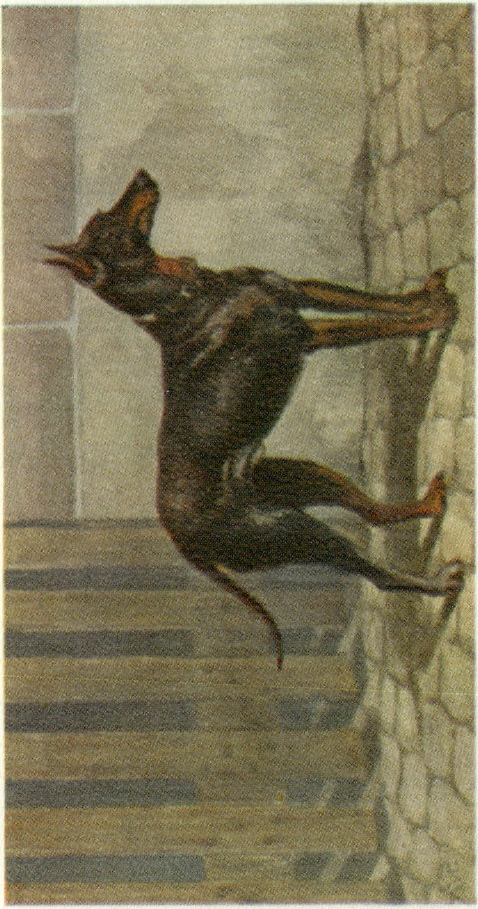

MASTIFF

Origin **Britain**

The mastiff is a canine heavyweight. With its large, long body, a male can weigh from 85–100 kilograms. Its silhouette is striking and dissuasive to intruders. However, this dog has no hidden aggressiveness; it is sociable with both people and other animals. Phoenician merchants took it to the British Isles in the first millennium BC. The Romans, who invaded Britain in 55 BC, were so impressed by the animal's strength that they took it with them back to Rome. But their fate was not an enviable one: they were thrown into the arena to fight. The mastiff in Britain was given other tasks, such as hunting large game, guarding villages and castles, and war. The mastiff's physique gradually became adapted to its different missions. After the Second World War, this dog had little place in society and came close to dying out. The British, who were still very attached to this breed – with its short, thick coat with coarse hair over the shoulders – sought out foreign stock with which to revive it. Today, the mastiff's coat is fawn or brindled, and it has black ears and mask. The mastiff is a dog that is as happy as can be when in contact with people.

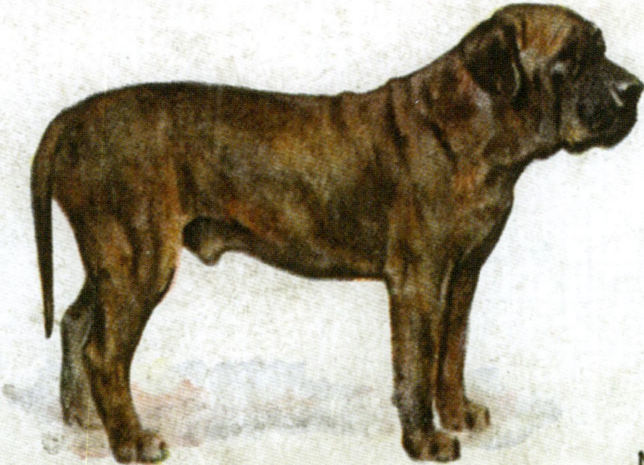

MASTIFF

IBIZAN HOUND

Origin **Spain (Balearic Islands)**

The Ibizan hound lives in the Balearic Islands, where it is known as the ca eivissenc. Living on islands has no doubt allowed it to preserve the primitive appearance of its ancestor, the tesem. This now-extinct Egyptian dog was a hunting dog similar to a greyhound. It was often depicted in ancient Egyptian tombs and, according to some, was the inspiration for the image of the god Anubis, who guided the souls of the dead. There is little doubt that Phoenician merchants introduced it to the Balearic Islands in the seventh century BC. The islanders immediately used it to hunt rabbits and hares, which it pursued as part of a pack. Both at night and during the day, the Ibizan hound would easily catch its quarry after tapping the dry soil with its paw to flush it out. In its quest, it would make more use of its excellent senses of hearing and smell than its sight. The Ibizan hound has a fine and long head; its ears are stiff and very mobile; and its amber eyes gleam with intelligence. Its hair is smooth, rough and, less often, long. Its coat mainly coloured red and white, entirely white or entirely red. The Ibizan hound is an independent and sometimes reserved dog, but a very patient one. It is always faithful to a loving master.

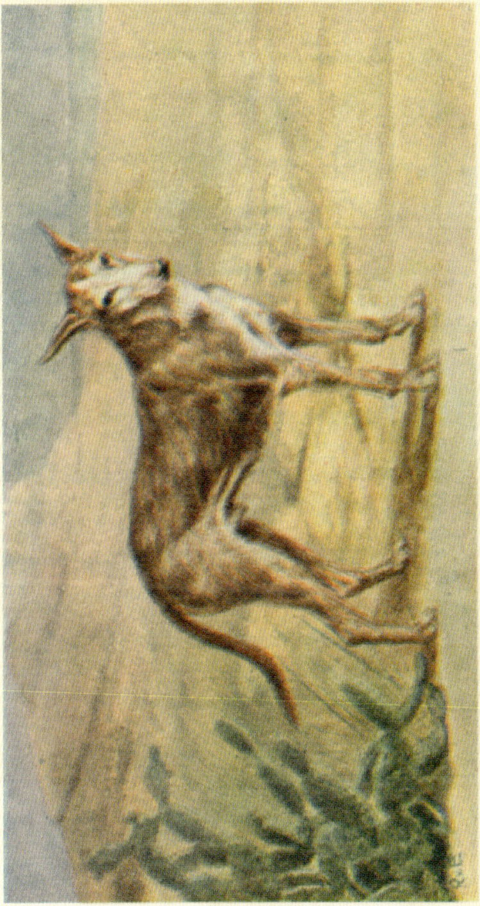

ENGLISH POINTER

Origin **Britain**

The cradle of this British breed is Portugal. At the origin of this dog, the Portuguese pointer was a tireless and fast dog that hunted with its nose in the air. The British crossed it with other breeds in order to produce a light and elegant dog. As a result, the English pointer made its first real appearance at the start of the seventeenth century. It is mainly used to hunt birds. It moves very quickly, then stops immediately in front of its quarry in a pointing stance once it has spotted it. Dog lovers consider this stop spectacular. The animal resembles a statue, with its head held high, body rigid, muscles tensed, tail immobile and positioned as a prolongation of its back, while only an instant earlier it would wag eagerly from side to side. The English pointer is a good-natured dog. It is gentle, kind and affectionate, and it needs to burn off the energy it has inherited from its ancestors. It loves wide open spaces. This medium-sized dog has a short, fine and smooth hair. Its coat can be orange and white, liver and brown, black and white, or lemon and white. It has hazel or brown eyes. Its slightly concave muzzle gives it an elegant upturned nose.

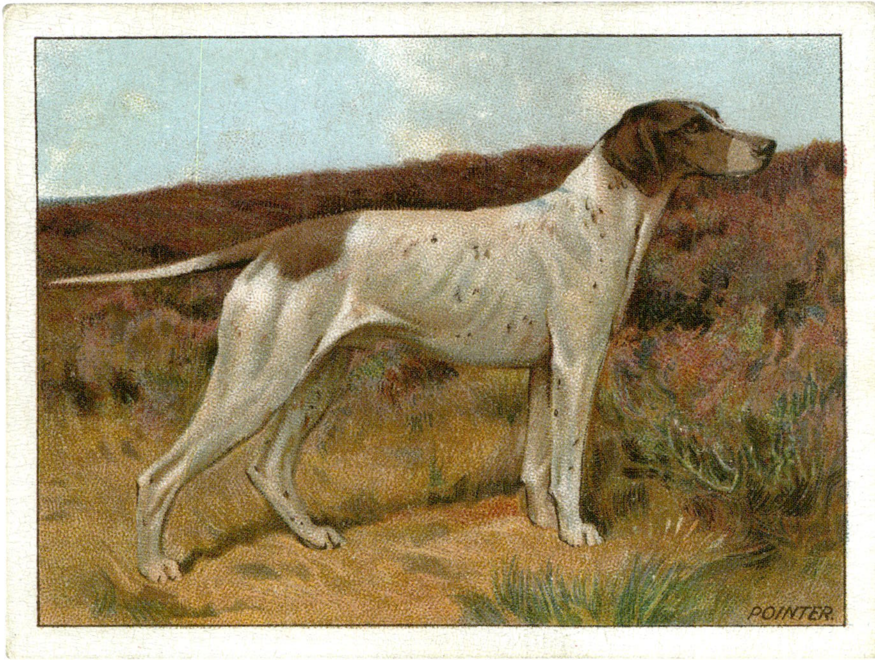
POINTER.

POITEVIN
Origin **France**

The Poitevin has an eventful history. In the nineteenth century, Viscount Émile de la Besge decided to form a pack of hounds with which to hunt wolves. To do this, he found a few specimens of ancient breeds in the local Haut-Poitou region. These offspring of hunting dogs had survived the disappearance of the breeding kennels owned by the nobility at the time of the French Revolution. They were all descended from dogs that at one time or another had belonged to the hunting packs of the kings of France. In 1842, just as he had achieved his aim, the viscount saw his kennel decimated by an epidemic of rabies. The only dogs spared by the disease were one male and two females, which he then crossed with with English hounds to create the Poitevin. Today, this dog's silhouette is graceful and muscular. Its head is elongated and its muzzle is slender, and its coat is always tricolour: white with large black and orange patches. The untiring Poitevin packs now hunt quarry other than wolves: hares, deer and wild boar.

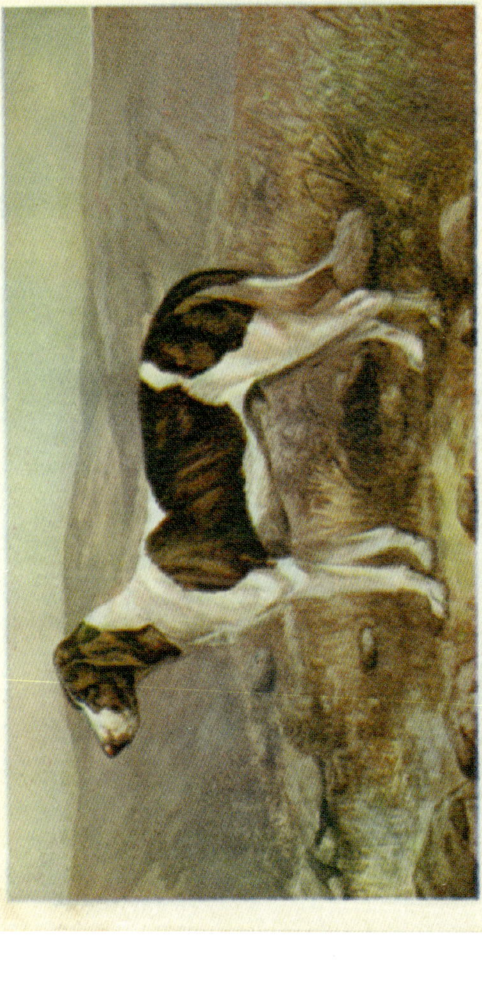

FLAT-COATED RETRIEVER

Origin **Britain**

This dog has inherited its abilities to retrieve and swim from its ancestor, the Saint John water dog. Originating in Newfoundland, the Saint John water dog was a faithful companion to Canadian fishermen in the seventeenth century. Its qualities were so appealing to the English gentry that they imported it to Britain in the nineteenth century. Saint John water dogs were used in hunts to retrieve game. They were later crossed with Irish setters and collies to improve their features. Their sense of smell was honed and their shaggy hair was flattened to give the appearance of the flat-coated retriever, which was first presented in a dog show in Birmingham in 1860. This retriever today has a black or liver coat with graceful feathering on its tail and legs. Its hair is dense, fine and as flat as possible. Its dark brown or hazel eyes gleam with intelligence and gentleness. Even when not hunting, this dog is always ready for outings and craves human company so much that it cannot cope with separation.

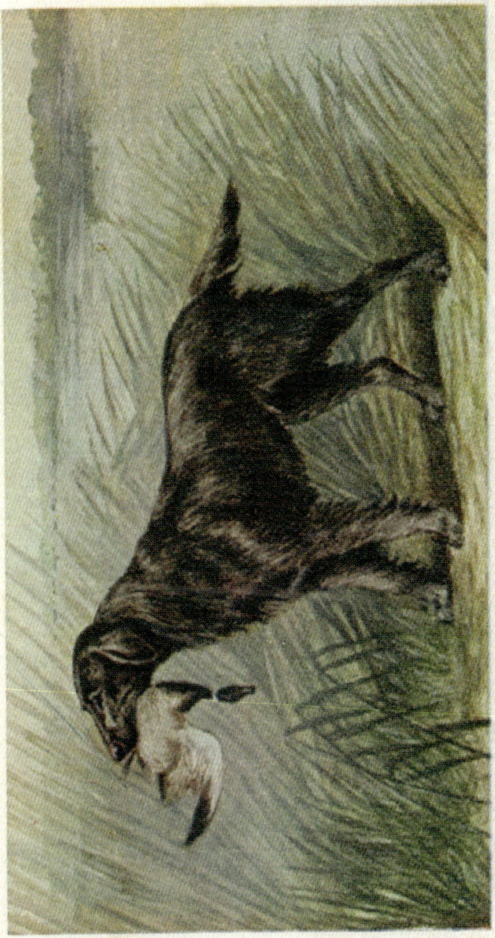

LABRADOR RETRIEVER

Origin **Britain**

The labrador retriever, known simply as the labrador, loves to live life to the fullest. This sturdy dog takes great pleasure in soft carpets, muddy marsh water, games and being fondled. Its great appetite can lead to its becoming overweight if nobody is attentive. This dog also loves to swim, which it carries in the blood. In fact, in the seventeenth century, its ancestors on the island of Newfoundland would jump into the water to help their masters, fishermen, bring fish onto their boats. At the time, Canadians named them Saint John water dogs, after the capital of the province of Newfoundland. In 1814 they crossed the Atlantic Ocean and arrived in the United Kingdom. The English gentry, who were passionate about dog breeds, took a great interest in the newcomers. They appreciated their instinct for retrieving. But it was in hunting, not fishing, where the qualities of those dogs were put to use by the aristocrats, and they were crossed with other hunting dogs. The breed standard was recognized by the Kennel Club, the official British canine organization, in 1903. Today, the labrador roams the marshes with its short, thick and dense coat, which can be black, yellow or brown. But its intelligence, patience, keen sense of smell and visual memory have led it to another fate. It has become an assistance dog, rescue dog and customs detection dog, as well as a joyful companion.

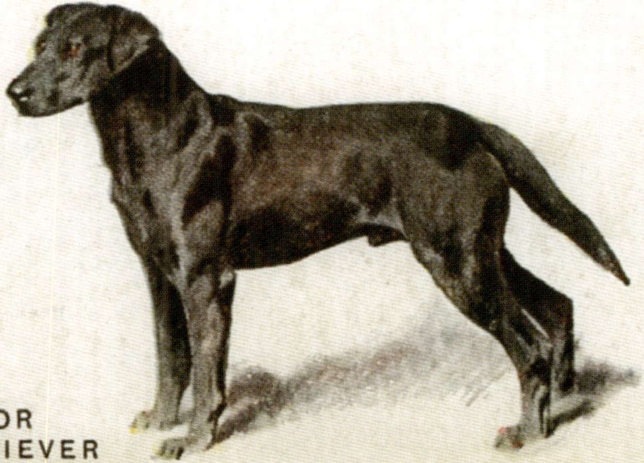

LABRADOR
RETRIEVER

ROTTWEILER
Origin **Germany**

In the year AD 73, the Romans invaded what is now the German state of Baden-Württemberg. The legions were accompanied by Molossian dogs, which were guard dogs and sheepdogs descended from the Tibetan mastiff. It was around what is now the town of Rottweil that those sturdy dogs mixed with native breeds, and the Rottweiler was born out of their union. Over the centuries, this dog was bred and used by German butchers to protect their property and livestock. It was also sometimes used as drafting dogs on farms or in mines. In the early twentieth century, the Rottweiler's excellent sense of smell, and its docility and strength drew the attention of police forces, who recruited them. Today, the Rottweiler combines strength, flexibility and resilience in the same squat body. A male can weigh about 50 kilograms and stand from 61–68 centimetres in height. It can be friendly and peaceful, but it is attentive to any new situation. It is faithful and loyal to its adoptive family, and will protect it. With its black coat with tan markings, the Rottweiler is a natural trotter. It has an honest, harmonious, strong and clean bearing. For a long time, they had their tails docked, but this is no longer permitted by law in many countries.

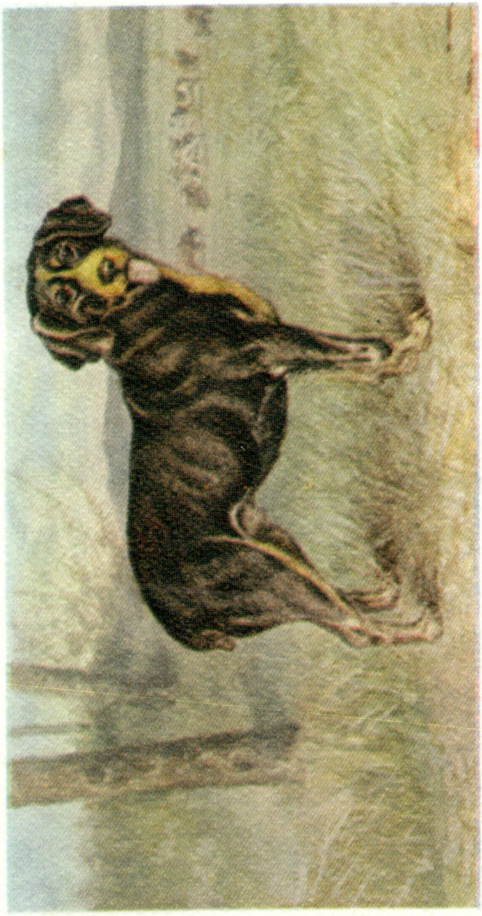

SAINT BERNARD

Origin **Switzerland**

The ancestor of the Saint Bernard originated in the upper region of Assyria, where bas-reliefs depict a dog closely resembling this Molossian dog. It then travelled with merchants and armies, first to Greece and then to Italy, before arriving in Switzerland, as evidenced by certain coats of arms of noble Swiss families in the fourteenth century that bear its head. In the seventeenth century it was found at the hospice on the Great Saint Bernard Pass. The monks entrusted it with the task of guarding and protecting, and this dog would soon accompany pilgrims over the pass. Above all, it would rescue travellers lost in the mountains and the fog. During the nineteenth century, the Saint Bernard would suffer from problems caused by inbreeding. The monks then decided to seek out robust Newfoundland dogs to strengthen their bloodline. The selective breeding was successful, and Saint Bernard breeding developed all over Europe. The Saint Bernard today has a friendly temperament. It can be a little stubborn, but this big-hearted dog loves family life.

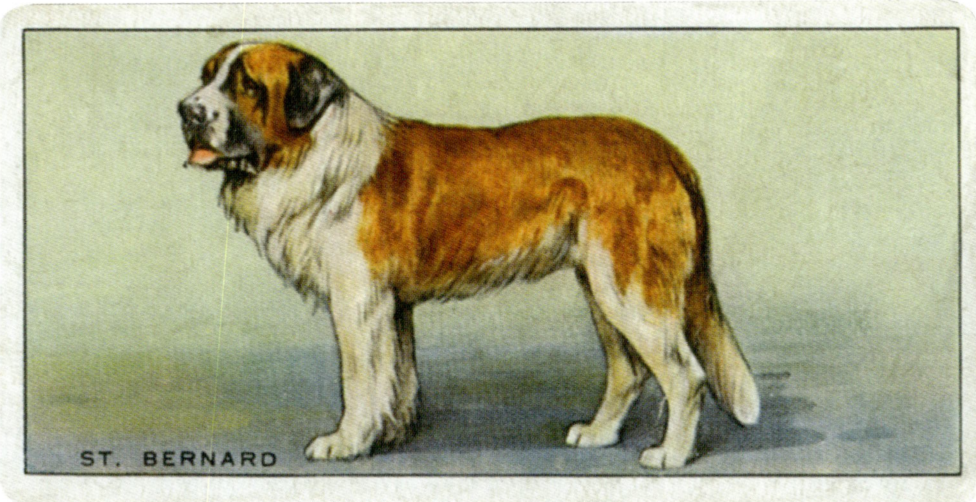
ST. BERNARD

SALUKI

Origin **Middle East**

'Son of the desert', 'desert eye' and 'wind drinker': Arabian tribes gave their salukis as many names as they did their thoroughbred horses. They prized the bravery, speed and stamina of those dogs, which for centuries they used for hunting. This Middle Eastern sighthound tirelessly pursued rabbits, hares and gazelles over sand and rocks across the desert, making use more of their sight than their sense of smell. The territories it has had to cross and the climate it has had to withstand gave rise to different varieties. There are two varieties today, one with feathering and a smooth variety without it. All salukis have a short, smooth and silky coat. Certain specimens have elegant feathering on their ears, tail and back of the legs. This hound was so precious that it was never sold, but sometimes given as a gift. This is how the first salukis made their appearance in Britain in about 1840. Nevertheless, the breed was not recognized until 1923. They became known in France ten years later, where this breed is still rare. The saluki does not hunt as much as it did in its homeland, but it continues to run after lures at greyhound tracks or in coursing sports. Its long and narrow head gives it a noble presence. Its large, oval eyes are dark brown or hazel, and its expression is sharp and profound. In Europe, it makes a gentle companion dog, even in cities, provided it can be allowed to burn off its energy. Its independent temperament is loved by its masters.

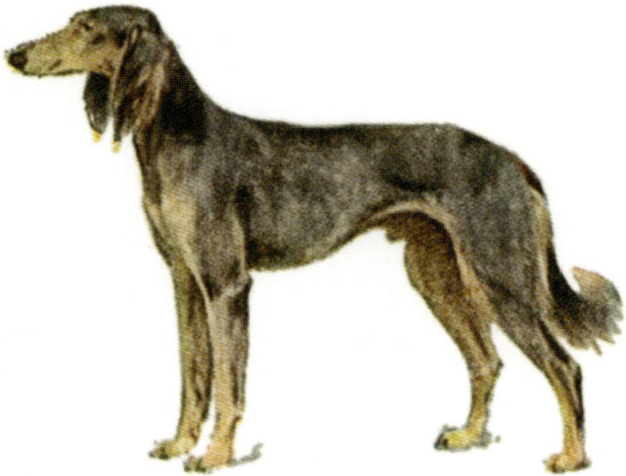

SALUKI

SAMOYED

Origin **Northern Russia and Siberia**

For hundreds of years, these primitive dogs accompanied nomadic Samoyed tribes through Siberia and northern Russia. In the north of their territory they were used as sledge dogs and hunting dogs. These dogs of gentle temperament had snow-white coat; in the south, their coat was white, black, or brown-spotted. In this region, their role was to guard herds of reindeer. In 1889, the zoologist Ernest Kilburn Scott brought back a specimen of the breed to Britain after spending three months with the Samoyed people. He repeated the operation on a second journey. These dogs, and others brought back by explorers, are the origin of the western Samoyed strain. European breeders preferred a light coat for this excellent companion dog. As a result, the Samoyed is pure white, cream, or white with biscuit, depending on the breed standard. Its lips, nose and the edges of its eyelids are black. It has abundant, thick, soft and dense hair that forms a coat which can withstand the Arctic cold. The Samoyed has sparkling eyes, reflecting its liveliness, gentleness and intelligence.

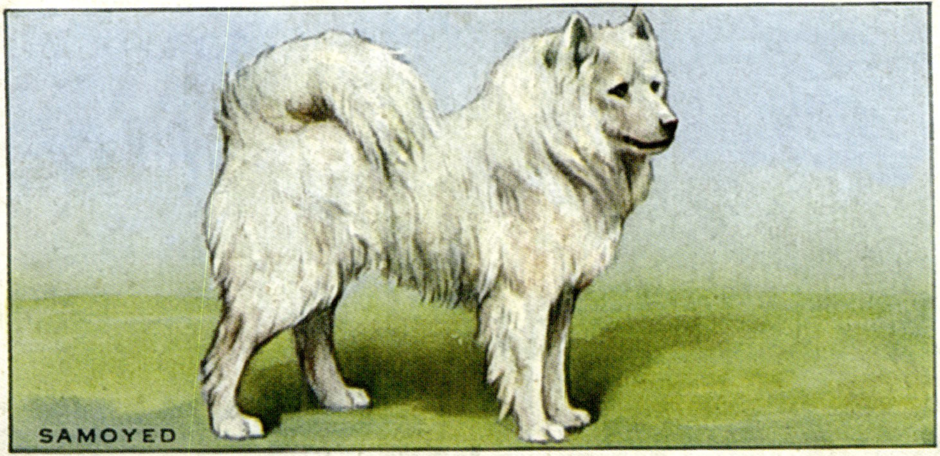
SAMOYED

SCHIPPERKE

Origin **Belgium**

Mice, rats, moles... no pests have ever escaped this little black sheepdog. Originating in Belgium, the schipperke had such excellent qualities as a ratter that it was adopted by people of modest means in the seventeenth century. At the time, cobblers in the Saint-Géry neighbourhood of Brussels even held beauty competitions for their dogs, which were adorned with magnificent, intricately decorated copper collars. Schipperke dogs did not have tails then, because their masters docked them. Docking has been banned in Belgium since 2006, and people let nature do its work – schipperkes are born either with or without a tail. Despite its distant origins, the schipperke only competed in a dog show for the first time in 1882. Six years later, a breed club was founded in Belgium. Since that time, its members have continued to standardize the type. There are now several varieties of this dog, named according to its city of origin: Antwerp, Louvain or Brussels. The schipperke has a typical coat, which is solid black with a ruff, a mane and a frill, and culottes that cover the thighs. This 5-7-kilogram dog is brimming with vitality. It is inquisitive, energetic and cheerful in company.

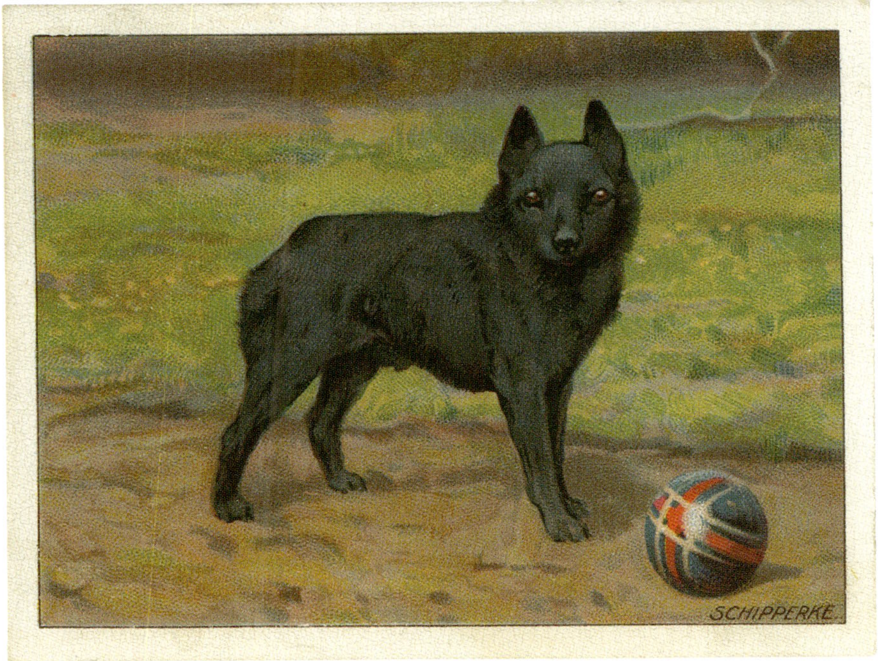
SCHIPPERKE.

SEALYHAM TERRIER

Origin **Britain**

The story of this terrier begins in nineteenth century in Sealyham, a village in the Welsh county of Pembrokeshire. It was the residence of Captain John Owen Tucker Edwardes, a Welshman who wanted to create the ideal terrier. He crossed and re-crossed the different terriers that existed at the time: the Welsh corgi, the Dandie Dinmont terrier, the bull terrier and the wire fox terrier, among others. He was ruthless in his selection of stock. He only kept the strongest specimens, which had to pass a battery of tests, particularly that of capturing rats or other pests. Before his death in 1891, Edwardes christened his terrier with the name of place of residence, Sealyham. It was first presented at a dog show in 1903. This modest-sized dog is longer than it is tall and has dark eyes. Its maximum height is 31 centimetres. Its hair is long, hard and wiry. Its coat is entirely white, or white with lemon, brown, blue or badger-pied markings. It has long been a custom to dock the tails of certain terriers, including this one. Always willing to play, the Sealyham has turned out to be a charming pet.

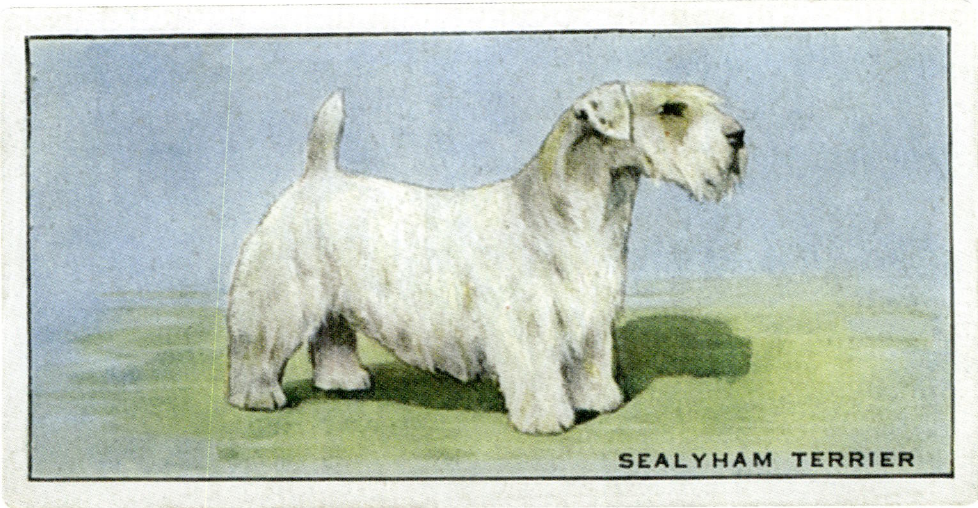
SEALYHAM TERRIER

ENGLISH SETTER

Origin **Britain**

This elegant breed is one of the oldest English hunting dogs. Its history in England dates back to the fourteenth century. Its ancestor is though to be the bird-dog, a spaniel used to hunt quail that originated in Spain. For centuries, the setter had another name, the 'setting' or crouching spaniel. It was used by hunters to capture game by net. After locating the birds, the dog would crouch without moving while it waited for its master to set nets and give the order to flush out the birds and drive them towards the trap. When net hunting was abandoned for the gun, the dog's name was changed to that of setter. In the nineteenth century, the Englishman Edward Laverack devoted more than fifty years to its selective breeding. Such was his influence that the black-and-white setter still bears his name. The setter has a silky coat with wavy hair and long feathering on the paws and tail. It can be blue belton (black and white), tricolour (black, white and orange), lemon (orange and white) or liver (brown and white). This very active dog makes a friendly, good-natured pet, but it remains a hunting dog.

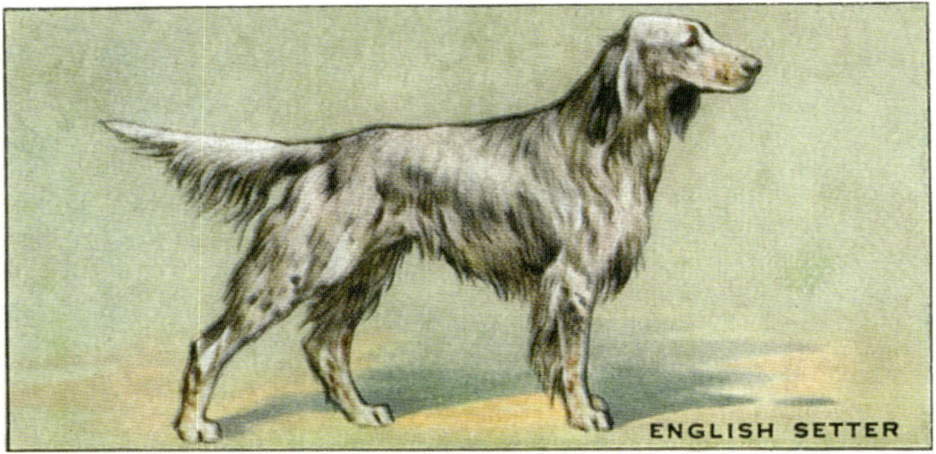
ENGLISH SETTER

IRISH RED SETTER

Origin **Ireland**

There are two varieties of Irish setters. Both make good companion dogs and hunting dogs. One has an entirely red coat, while the other has a red-and-white coat. The latter, although less well known, appears to be the older of the two. Its moment of hunting glory came in the seventeenth century, and its younger sibling appeared a century later. It was the result of crossing a white-and-red specimen with an unknown red dog. In the nineteenth century, dog lovers would mistake the two types of Irish setters at dog shows, which enthusiasts of the breed were not happy about, so a move was made to differentiate them. The red setter soon became more successful than its older sibling, to the extent that it was feared that the red-and-white setter would die out. The red Irish setter is often compared to a thoroughbred: its musculature is long and dense, and its skin is fine and taut. Its coat is rich autumnal chestnut in colour. It has short, fine-textured hair on its head, with finely feathered and silky hair on its ears, under the belly, on the chest and tail, and on the back of the legs. This aristocratic, athletic and friendly dog uses all its qualities when hunting. It is sometimes called the 'red devil' because of its great zeal. This gentle, affectionate and cheerful dog has won over families, to whom it is a faithful companion.

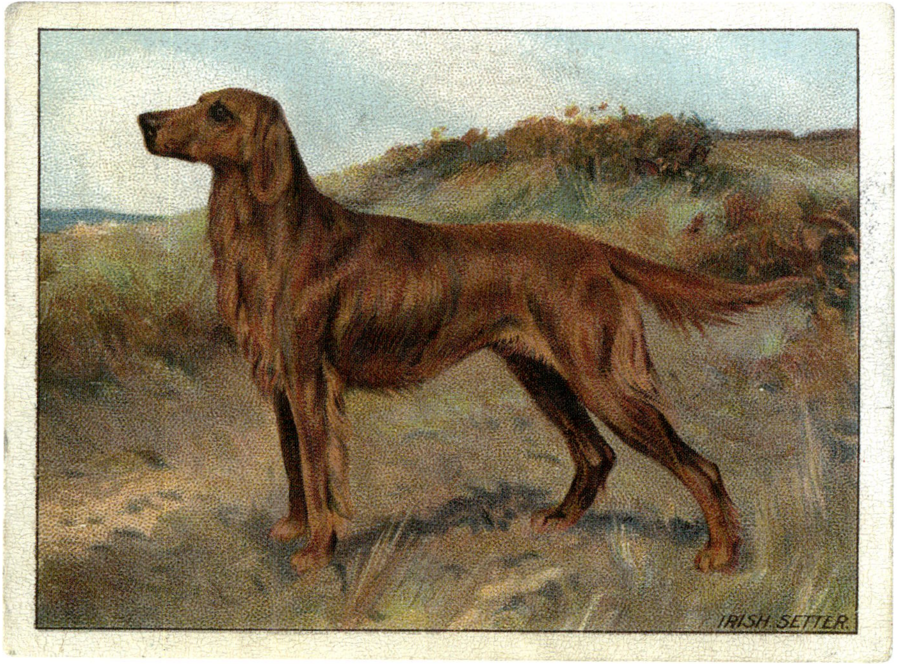
IRISH SETTER.

SKYE TERRIER

Origin **Britain**

Greyfriars Bobby was the most famous Skye terrier. He lived in Edinburgh in 1858, and when his master died he sat on his grave. Although attempts were made to lead him away, he remained steadfast until his own death. This story is a perfect example of how a Skye terrier is the dog of only one master, and that is has a very strong character. Before it became a companion dog, it was used to hunt rats, foxes and badgers in homes and around farms. Its long hair falls as attractive feathering on over its ears, tail and face. It is the result of crossing terriers native to the coastal region of northwestern Scotland. The English monarchs soon became interested in this dog with eyes that sparkled with life and intelligence. First was Queen Elizabeth I, in the sixteenth century, then Queen Victoria, in the nineteenth century. However, its glory has not stood the test of time, and the Skye terrier is very rare today.

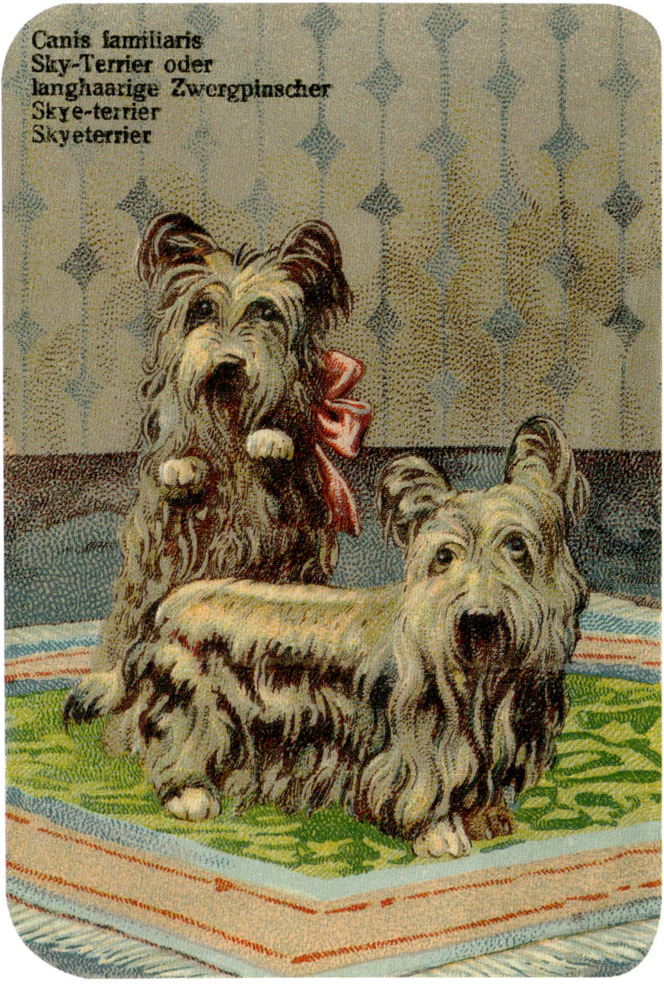
Canis familiaris
Sky-Terrier oder
langhaarige Zwergpinscher
Skye-terrier
Skyeterrier

DUTCH SMOUSHOND

Origin **Netherlands**

Under the coarse, harsh and almost unkempt coat of the smoushond, there is a heart of gold. This cheerful and friendly dog feels at ease anywhere, especially with a family, where it can give free rein to affection, which is seen in its kind and lively expression. As far as its origins are concerned, dog lovers are not exactly sure. Could its ancestors have been yellow schnauzers? The smoushond was known to have been very popular in the nineteenth century with Dutch gentlemen. Like the Dalmatian, the Dutch smoushond was a carriage dog or gentleman's stable dog and would run alongside carriages. At home, it would hunt rats and other rodents. The smoushond breed club was founded in the Netherlands in 1905. But this energetic and muscular breed gradually went into decline. In the 1970s, two enthusiasts decided to revive its breeding. Their efforts have only recently begun to bear fruit. However, the breeders prefer that their dogs do not cross any borders to leave the Netherlands, because the situation is still precarious. The smoushond is practically unknown in France. By 2009, the Société Centrale Canine had not recorded a single one in its French breed registry.

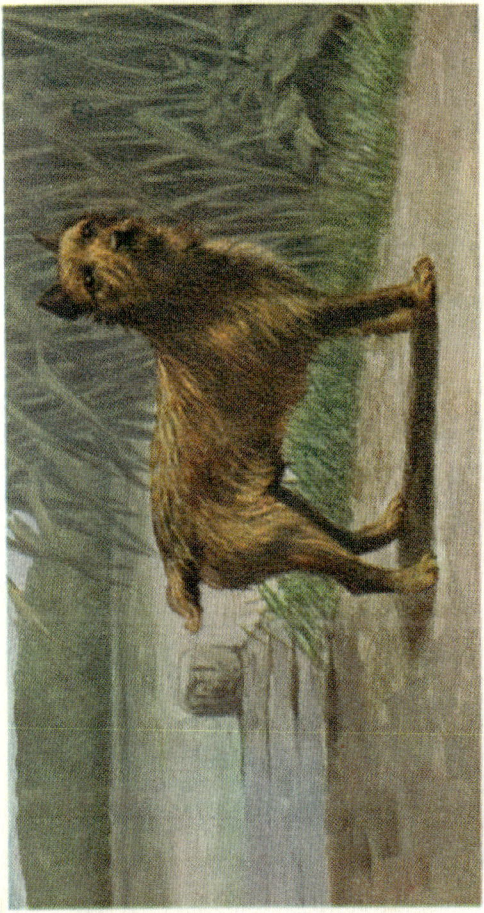

GERMAN SPITZ

Origin **Germany**

There are five different types of German spitz. Their dimensions and coats differ from one variety to another. The keeshond or wolfspitz is the largest. It can grow to 49 centimetres in height, and its coat is always wolf grey. The toy spitz, also known as the Pomeranian, is the smallest. It can measure about 20 centimetres. All spitzes belong to the same breed, which is the oldest in central Europe. It descends from the stone age 'peat dogs' (Canis familiaris palustris rüthimeyer) and lake dwellers' dogs. In the nineteenth century, Queen Victoria showed interest in the toy spitz, which led to its becoming fashionable in Britain. Its nickname is 'pom' or 'pompom'. The physique of this dog has great appeal, with its abundant hair forming an opulent mane around its neck and shoulders, and its bushy tail cheerfully curled over its back. There is also no doubt that its fine, fox-like muzzle and lively dark eyes will both surprise and delight. The spitz is a frisky dog that is attentive to its family. It is always on the alert with strangers, but it becomes neither aggressive nor fearful.

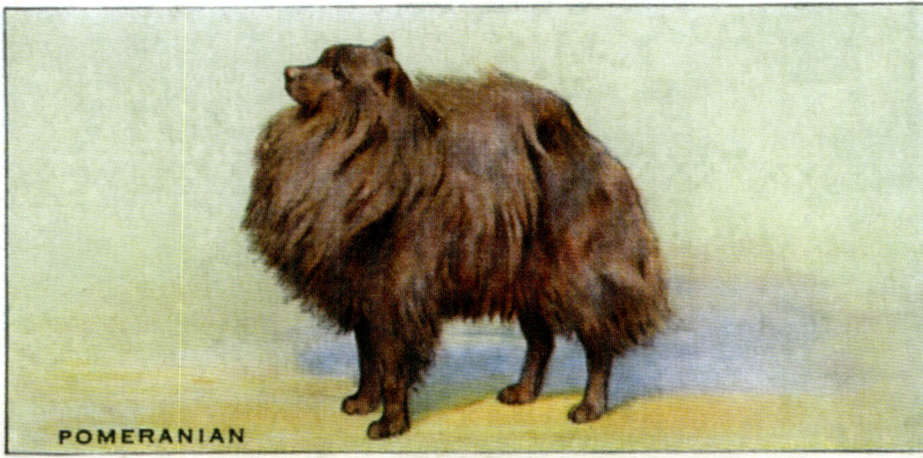
POMERANIAN

DACHSHUND

Origin **Germany**

The graceful way a dachshund walks on a lead would make anybody forget that this dog is a brave and determined hunter that is used for all kinds of hunting styles. Its qualities allow it, at will, to take the role of terrier, flushing dog, scenthound... or attentive and joyful companion dog. This breed has been known in Germany since the Middle Ages. It was descended from brachet, basset or short-legged hunting dogs, because the dachshund has short legs and a long body. There are three varieties of dachshund (smooth-haired, wire-haired and long-haired), and they come in three sizes and with more than three coat colours. The standard dachshund weighs less than 9 kilograms; the miniature dachshund weighs about 4 kilograms; and the 'rabbit' size dachshund weighs 3.5 kilograms. The smooth-haired dachshund is the oldest variety. In the sixteenth century, it was crossed with a spaniel to create the long-haired variety. The result of this union was a gentle and affectionate dog. The wire-haired dachshund appeared in the nineteenth century. It is believed to have the genes of a schnauzer, Dandie Dinmont terrier and a Scottish terrier. It also has a strong-willed temperament. The affectionate and cheerful dachshund also has a possessive, even jealous, streak. While it is at home in the city, it still needs to burn off energy in a natural setting.

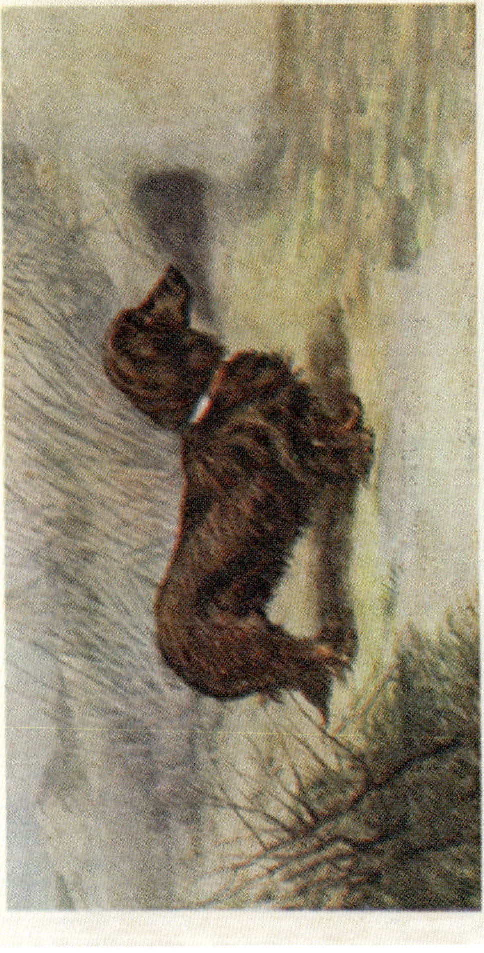

NEWFOUNDLAND

Origin **Canada**

Like that of other dog breeds, the Newfoundland's tail expresses joy, anxiety and questioning, but it also serves another purpose. The large tail with strong base is also used as a rudder. This imposing animal is in fact an excellent swimmer, both in rivers and the sea. The Newfoundland is so at home in the water that it has been trained to be a water rescue dog, hence the nickname 'Saint Bernard of the sea'. While there is no doubt about its bravery, its origins paint a different story. The most commonly accepted genealogy puts its roots on the island of Newfoundland. It was thought to be the result of crossing native dogs and the large black bear dog introduced by the Vikings to the island in about 1100. In the sixteenth century, it was crossed with the dogs of European cod fisherman who sailed off the Canadian coast. At the time, this breed had many tasks: it was a pack or drafting animal, guard dog, hunting dog or rescue dog. Its silhouette is clearly defined. Noble, joyful and enterprising, the Newfoundland, whether black, black-and-white or brown, makes a formidable companion for life.

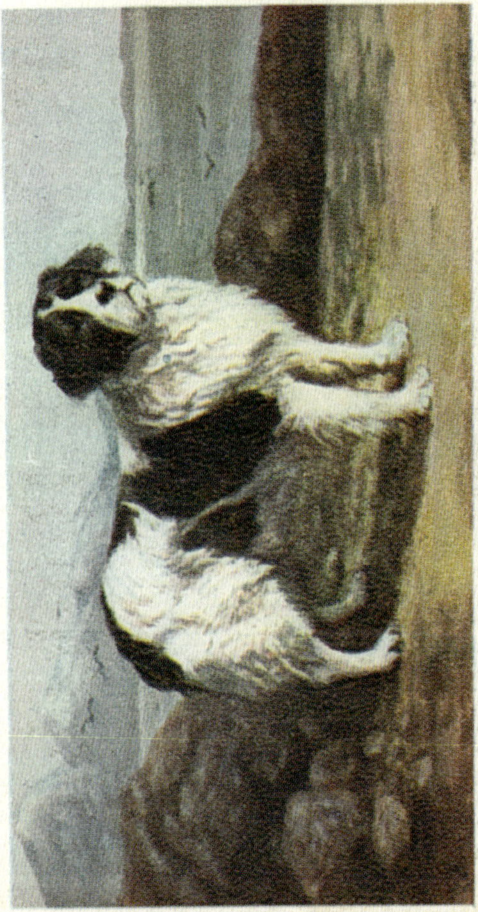

BOSTON TERRIER

Origin **United States**

This dog is nicknamed the 'American gentleman', a reflection of how enthusiasts of the breed describe its neat silhouette and the gentleness and cheerfulness it demonstrates to its family. The Boston terrier makes an adorable pet. This intelligent, affectionate, playful and sporting dog is even-tempered. However, like many terriers, this sociable and balanced dog requires a lot of attention. Its ancestry is well known. An individual was imported into the United States from Britain with the name of Judge, and was purchased in 1865 by the Boston resident Robert C. Cooper. The animal was the result of crossing a bulldog with a now-extinct white English terrier. Its coat was dark and brindled and it had a white blaze on its head. It weighed about 14 kilograms. Judge was mated with a white-haired female that was lighter and had shorter legs. Their descendants were given the name of 'round heads' until the founding of the Boston Terrier Club, the breed club, in 1891. Today there are three weight categories for these terriers. The heaviest can reach 25 pounds, or 11.35 kilograms. The Boston terrier's coat has kept Judge's colouring, brindled seal with white markings on head and chest.

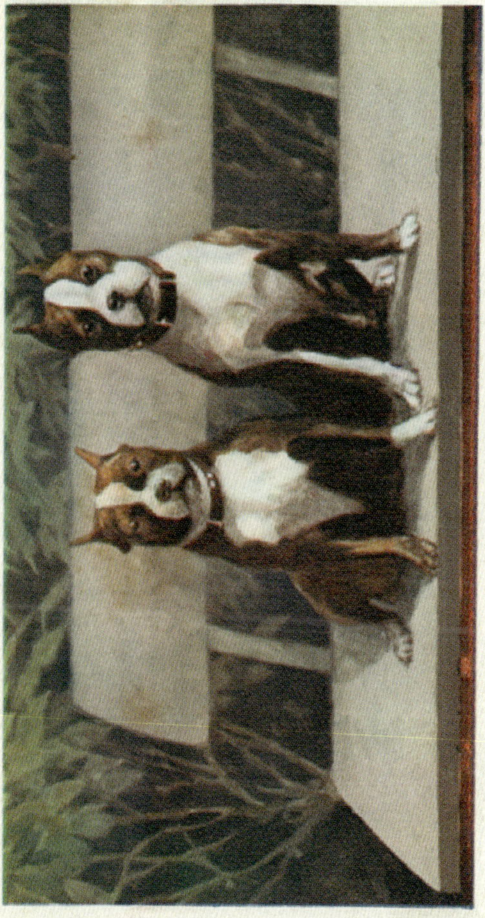

IRISH TERRIER

Origin **Ireland**

'The poor man's sentinel, the farmer's friend and the gentleman's favourite' is how the Irish terrier has been charmingly described. The Irish terrier is one of the four terrier breeds originating in Ireland, and is undoubtedly one of the oldest. Before the 1880s, it could have a red coat, but also black-and-tan or a brindled one. Subsequently, breeders gave precedence to a coat with the colours red, red wheaten or yellow-red. It was with this red coat that the Irish terrier entered its first dog shows in the early twentieth century. The four Irish breeds developed a silhouette that was differentiated from that of other European terriers. The Irish terrier is muscular and sinewy, with elegant lines. It is fast, resilient and strong. Such qualities allowed it become a messenger dog in the horror of trench warfare during the First World War. It has a long head and sparkles with fire. Its tail is quite long and carried gaily. In countries where it is permitted, it is still being docked today. This breed has a dense and wiry coat, and its muzzle is adorned with a slight beard. The Irish terrier measures about 45 centimetres at the withers. And the ultimate quality: it is faithful at all times and loves taking part in family life.

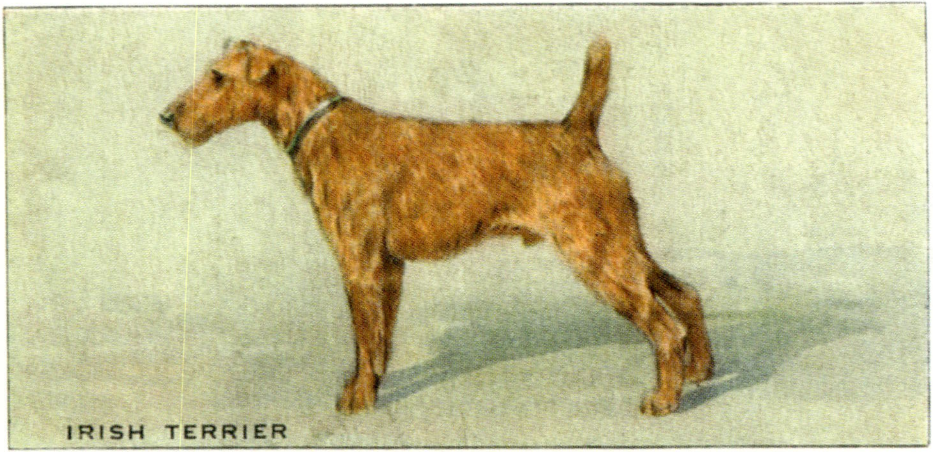
IRISH TERRIER

KERRY BLUE TERRIER

Origin **Ireland**

This terrier started out as a rat catcher. It was also an all-round farm dog. With these humble origins, there is no trace of it in canine annals. The first texts that mention this breed only date from 1847, describing a bluish, slate-coloured dog with dark blotches and patches, often with tan about the legs and muzzle. The Irish claim to have known about it for centuries, and County Kerry was possibly its cradle. However, the first specimen was only presented in a show in 1913. Seven years later, a breed club was founded in Dublin. Between the two world wars, the Kerry blue terrier became the mascot for the Irish nationalists during their war of independence and its reputation soon spread beyond the island and around the world. The Kerry blue is a pure-bred terrier, in both temperament and silhouette. It has a soft and wavy coat. Kerry blue puppies are black or fawn, but as an adult it turns a bluish shade, with or without black points. This expressive dog carries its tail erect. It is very affectionate, although it can sometimes prove to be stubborn, like many terriers. It has become a very prized companion for family life, but there are still some that continue to hunt for rats and otters in deep water.

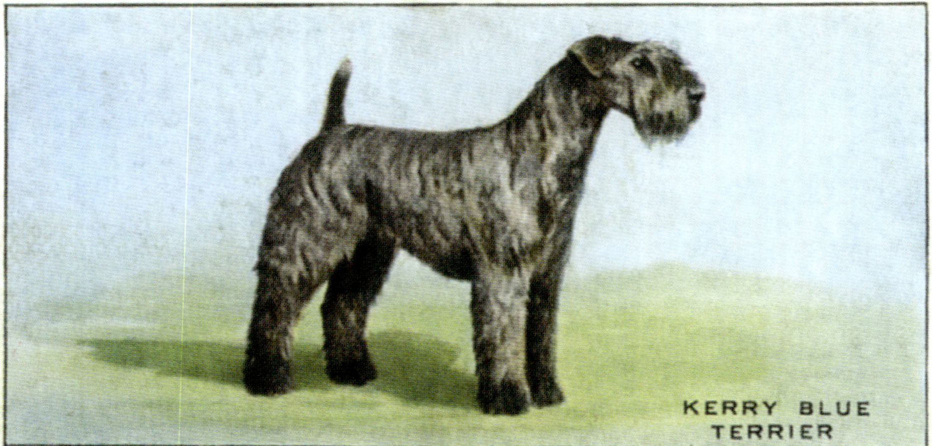
KERRY BLUE
TERRIER

WHIPPET

Origin **Britain**

Before there was a name for a single breed of sighthounds, the term whippet was used to refer to all small and fast dogs in Britain. The whippet today, however, is not small; the male measures from 47–51 centimetres. But it is fast. There are still many grey areas in the whippet's genealogy, even though for centuries England has been home to dogs resembling it. It may well be that greyhounds, dogs of the England's medieval aristocracy, were the ancestors of the whippet. Certain dog enthusiasts also suggest cross-breeding with terriers. The first people to show interest in them were miners of the Midlands and northern regions of England. In the seventeenth century, they held races featuring these strong and graceful dogs. In those regions, whippet racing remained more popular than greyhound racing until the First World War. Since whippets sprinted over short distances, they often trained in city lanes. Certain dogs were able to run 180 metres in 12 seconds. This dog has short, fine and close hair. No colour is imposed by the breed standard, which is an exception among canine breeds. This sensitive, intelligent and very affectionate dog loves the affection shown by humans, and its quiet charm has managed to seduce many.

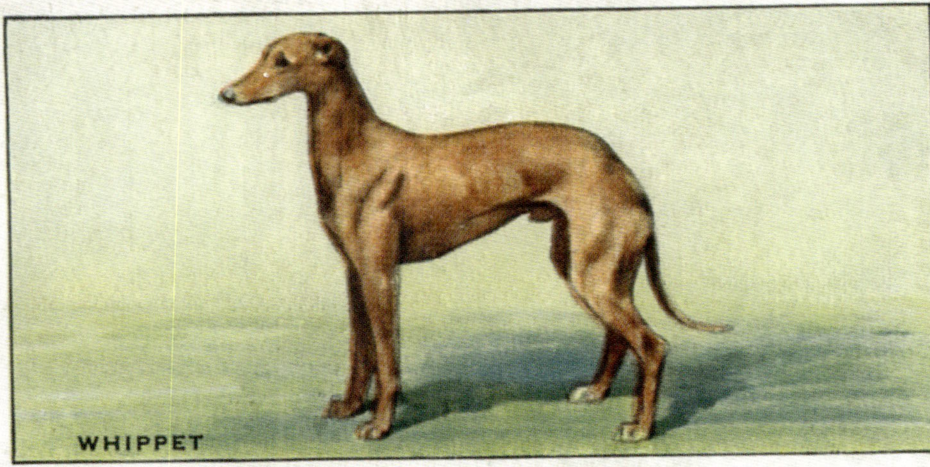

WHIPPET

LIST OF DOGS BY BREED TYPE

Name	Breed type
Appenzeller cattle dog	pinscher and schnauzer, molossoid breeds, Swiss mountain and cattle dogs
Ariège pointer	pointers
Basenji	spitz and primitive types
Basset hound	hounds, scenthounds and related breeds
Beagle	small-sized hounds
Bedlington terrier	terriers
Bloodhound	hounds, scenthounds and related breeds
Blue Gascony Basset	hounds, scenthounds and related breeds
Borzoi	sighthounds
Boston terrier	companion and toy dogs
Bourbonnais pointer	pointers
Bull terrier	terriers
Bulldog	pinscher and schnauzer, molossoid breeds, Swiss mountain and cattle dogs, and other breeds
Bullmastiff	pinscher and schnauzer, molossoid breeds, Swiss mountain and cattle dogs
Cairn terrier	terriers
Canadian Eskimo	working dogs (Canadian classification)
Chow chow	spitz and primitive types, Asian spitz and related breeds

Name	Breed type
Clumber spaniel	retrievers, flushing dogs, water dogs
Corded poodle	companion and toy dogs
Dachshund	dachshunds
Dalmatian	hounds, scenthounds and related breeds
Dandie Dinmont terrier	terriers
Deerhound	sighthounds
Dobermann	pinscher and schnauzer, molossoid breeds, Swiss mountain and cattle dogs
Dogue de Bordeaux	pinscher and schnauzer, molossoid breeds, Swiss mountain and cattle dogs
Dupuy pointer	pointers
Dutch shepherd	sheepdogs and cattle dogs
Dutch smoushond	pinscher and schnauzer, molossoid breeds, Swiss mountain and cattle dogs
English cocker spaniel	flushing dogs
English pointer	pointers
English setter	pointers
English springer spaniel	retrievers, flushing dogs, water dogs
Flat-coated retriever	retrievers, flushing dogs, water dogs
Fox hound	hounds, scenthounds and related breeds
French bulldog	companion and toy dogs
French hound	hounds, scenthounds and related breeds
French pointer	pointers
French water dog	retrievers, flushing dogs, water dogs

Name	**Breed type**
German pointer	pointers
German shepherd	sheepdogs and cattle dogs
German spitz	spitz and primitive types
Golden retriever	retrievers, flushing dogs, water dogs
Great Dane	pinscher and schnauzer, molossoid breeds, Swiss mountain and cattle dogs
Greyhound	sighthounds
Griffon Nivernais	hounds, scenthounds and related breeds
Ibizan hound	spitz and primitive types
Irish red setter	pointers
Irish terrier	terriers
Japanese chin	companion and toy dogs
Kerry blue terrier	terriers
King Charles spaniel	companion and toy dogs
Labrador retriever	retrievers, flushing dogs, water dogs
Laika	spitz and primitive types
Leonberger	pinscher and schnauzer, molossoid breeds, Swiss mountain and cattle dogs
Maltese	companion and toy dogs
Manchester terrier	terriers
Mastiff	pinscher and schnauzer, molossoid breeds, Swiss mountain and cattle dogs
Mongrel	
Newfoundland	pinscher and schnauzer, molossoid breeds, Swiss mountain and cattle dogs

Name	Breed type
Old English sheepdog	sheepdogs and cattle dogs
Otterhound	hounds, scenthounds and related breeds
Pekingese	companion and toy dogs
Poitevin	hounds, scenthounds and related breeds
Poodle	companion and toy dogs
Rottweiler	pinscher and schnauzer, molossoid breeds, Swiss mountain and cattle dogs
Rough collie	sheepdogs and cattle dogs
Russian hound	hounds
Saint Bernard	pinscher and schnauzer, molossoid breeds, Swiss mountain and cattle dogs
Saluki	sighthounds
Samoyed	spitz and primitive types
Schipperke	sheepdogs and cattle dogs
Sealyham terrier	terriers
Skye terrier	terriers
Smooth fox terrier	terriers
South Russian shepherd	sheepdogs and cattle dogs
Swedish elkhound	spitz and primitive types
Whippet	sighthounds
Wire fox terrier	terriers
Xoloitzcuintli	spitz and primitive types

IN THE SAME COLLECTION IN FRENCH

The Little Book of Saints, Volume 1, Christine Barrely, Saskia Leblon, Laure Péraudin, Stéphane Trieulet

The Little Book of Saints, Volume 2, Defendente Génolini

The Little Book of the Bible, Christine Barrely

The Little Book of the Life of Jesus, Christine Barrely

The Little Book of Mary, Christine Barrely

The Little Book of Gods, Olivia Nour

The Little Book of Angels, Nicole Masson

The Little Book of Kings of France, Guillaume Picon, Katia Boudoyan

The Little Book of the French Revolution, Christine Barrely Jean-Claude and Josette Demory

The Little Book of Napoleon, David Chanteranne

The Little Book of French Departments, Nicole Masson

The Little Book of Towns and Coats of Arms, Marie-Odile Mergnac

The Little Book of Idiomatic Expressions, Dominique Foufelle

The Little Book of Cats, Brigitte Bulard-Cordeau (available in English)

The Little Book of Mushrooms, Myriam Blanc

The Little Book of Trees, Dominique Pen Du

The Little Book of Flowers, Dominique Pen Du

All images are from the private collection of Éditions du Chêne.

58, rue Jean Bleuzen CS 70007 92178 Vanves Cedex
www.editionsduchene.fr

Editorial Manager: Nathalie Bailleux, with the collaboration of Franck Friès
Editorial Assistant: Fanny Martin
Art Director: Sabine Houplain
Proofreading: Myriam Blanc
Production: Marion Lance

Printed by Toppan Printing
In China
Copyright Registration: April 2019
ISBN : 978-2-81231-858-0
29/0992/3-02